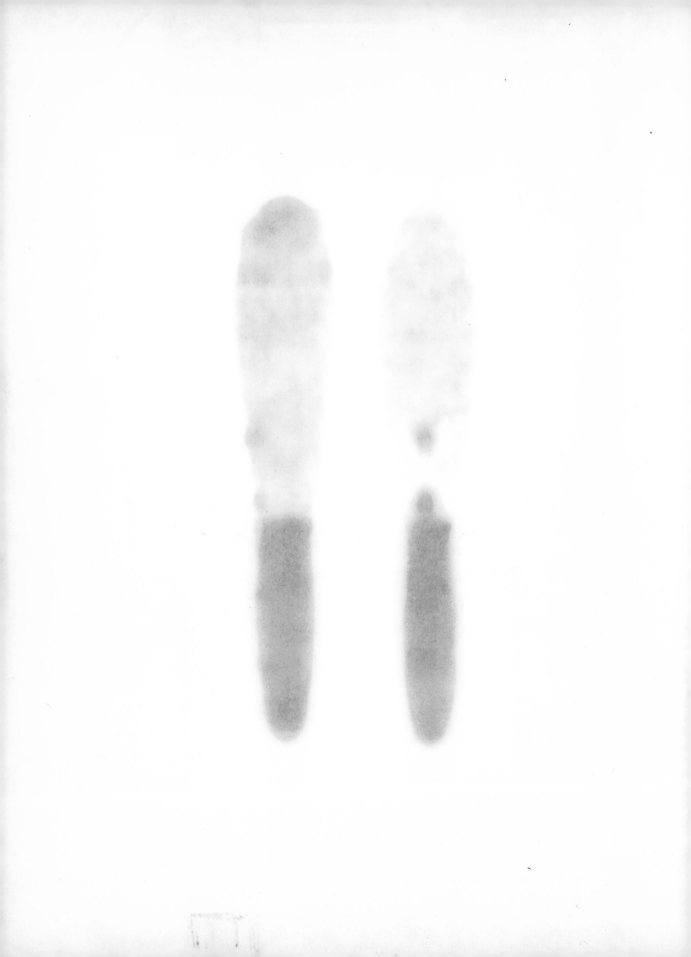

A PICTORIAL HISTORY
OF THE
GREAT COMEDIANS

A PICTORIAL HISTORY OF THE GREAT COMEDIANS

BY WILLIAM CAHN

An up-to-date version of what was published originally as *The Laugh Makers—A Pictorial History of American Comedians*

GROSSET & DUNLAP, INC.
A NATIONAL GENERAL COMPANY
Publishers   •   New York

To Rhoda

Introduction

There are many ways of looking at comedy.

A psychiatrist: "The urge to laugh, in civilized man, seems to be almost as irrepressible as the urges of hunger and sex."

A zoo keeper: "When a chimp is playful and happy, it does not smile as we do."

A comedian: "Humor is one of the best safety valves."

A night-club owner: "I mean, what the hell is there to laugh at . . . People see nothing funny in pollution, over-population and Viet Nam."

A great newspaper: "Our age desperately needs fun and nonsense."

An anthropologist: "When you have people who cannot laugh at people in power —then you're in trouble."

Another comedian: "Somehow slipping on a banana peel *is* funny."

There are many points of view. For example, mine:

Laughter is a bond of friendship which can help unite the past with the present; and people of all languages, ages and points of view.

William Cahn

Table of Contents

1

He Made George Washington Laugh

"Vot iss id has two feet, has fedders all ofer id, und barks like a dog?"
"I give up."
"A chicgen."
"Why, a chicken doesn't bark like a dog!"
"I know id; I chust pud id in to make id hard!"

People laughed at Sam Bernard's comedy of a past generation.

But no comedian is ever dead certain what makes an audience laugh.

Laughing is the expression of merriment by convulsive sounds accompanied by opening the mouth and wrinkling the face.

People laughed when W. C. Fields solemnly explained away his drinking habits by saying that he didn't believe in "dining on an empty stomach."

They laughed when Gracie Allen explained that the reason why she drives with the emergency brake on is in case there is an emergency.

They laughed, too, at Henry Morgan's story of how he was born of mixed parents. His mother was a woman and his father was a man.

The first professional comedian in our nation's history was Tom Wignell, a man little known today but quite a joker in his time. Wignell appeared in the first native American comedy in 1787.

[*Facsimile, slightly reduced*]

G. Washington

THE

CONTRAST,

A

COMEDY;

IN FIVE ACTS:

WRITTEN BY A

CITIZEN OF THE *UNITED STATES;*

Performed with Applause at the Theatres in NEW-YORK,
PHILADELPHIA, and MARYLAND;

AND PUBLISHED *(under an Assignment of the Copy-Right)* BY

THOMAS WIGNELL.

Primus ego in patriam
Aonio———deduxi vertice Musas.
                                        VIRGIL.
(*Imitated.*)
First on our shores I try THALIA's powers,
And bid the *laughing, useful* Maid be ours.

PHILADELPHIA:

FROM THE PRESS OF *PRICHARD & HALL,* IN MARKET STREET,
BETWEEN SECOND AND FRONT STREETS.

M. DCC. XC.

The first native American comedy was *The Contrast*. George Washington enjoyed going to the theater and was a fan of Thomas Wignell (below) the first major American comedian. The copy of *The Contrast* (left) was the personal possession of Washington, whose signature appears on it.

From its beginning, the drama in America has had a difficult time of it. When some English actors tried to organize a theater in New England back in 1750, there was a small riot and the Massachusetts General Court sternly reaffirmed its traditional ban on "public stage plays, interludes and other theatrical entertainments."

With the Puritanical finger leveled in their direction the theaters that existed found the going difficult. Small wonder that it was hard to squeeze a laugh from them. Except for Shakespeare, most of the plays were second-rate imitations of foreign import, many derived from England.

Further trouble resulted in 1774 when the Continental Congress ordered the closing of all places of public amusement. There was a revolution to be won. The edict was against "horse racing, and all kinds of gamery, cock fighting, exhibitions of shews, plays, and other expensive Diversions and Entertainments."

A dozen years later, however, the reopened theater was ripe for comedy. This probably accounts for the reception given to the play *The Contrast* by Royall Tyler which held up to ridicule "corrupt and frivolous practices of the old world of fashion contrasted with the sturdy, vigorous forthrightness of new America."

It was the first American play produced by an American, written by an American, played by Americans with an American theme. The main character in the play was Jonathan, a humorous Yankee servant, played by Wignell.

Although *The Contrast* was given to much talking and little action, it was well received by the theatergoing public in the small, slowly growing city of New York, and played five times in quick succession.

Wignell, who came to America from England at the outbreak of the Revolutionary War, was a man below ordinary height with a slight stoop of the shoulder. According to William Dunlap, the pioneer theatrical historian whose scrutiny of an actor was thorough: "Wignell was athletic with handsomely formed lower extremities, the knees a little curved inward, and feet remarkably small. His large blue eyes were rich in expression, and his comedy was luxuriant in humor, but always faithful to his author. He was a comic actor, not a buffoon."

Taking the part of a low-comedy servant, Wignell would shuffle about the stage whittling sticks, ejaculating frequently "Tarnation" or "I vum" and calling himself "the true-born son of liberty." Wignell's characterization of Jonathan, the shrewd, half-educated Yankee servant, was to set a pattern for future Jonathans for many years to come.

With these and other roles Wignell attracted the attention of no less a personage than President George Washington, a devoted fan of the theater. Perhaps Tom Wignell's career reached its highest point on the night of November 24, 1789, when a play, *Poor Soldier,* in which he was the main comic character, was presented to the public. There was a great furor when it was learned that a party including President Washington had made reservations for the evening performance. Special preparations were made to receive the beloved hero of the Revolutionary War.

According to the records of the time, Washington sat very stiff and stern in his box

Joseph Jefferson I was one of our first popular comedians and helped continue the Yankee character originated by Tom Wignell. He is pictured above (left) in a scene from an early play, *A Budget of Blunders.*

watching the comedy. When the final curtain fell and the President gave not the slightest indication of having been amused, Wignell took the opportunity of a curtain call to present a brief and flowery verse dedicated to the first President.

The poem described Washington as "a man who fought to free the land from woe," etc. As the reading approached its conclusion, Washington remained as stiff and stern as before, perhaps stiffer.

Wignell sensed the possible embarrassment felt by the honored guest at too much praise on his night off. Cleverly he contrived for a fellow actor to ask:

"How look'd he . . . was he tall or short?"

Wignell answered:

> "Why sure, I didn't see him. To be sure,
> As I was looking hard from out the door
> I saw a man in regimentals fine,
> All lace and glitter, botherum and shine;
> And so I look'd at him till all was gone,
> And then I found that he was not the one."

Washington burst into a hearty laugh.

Wignell had become the first comedian — but by no means the last — to make a President laugh.

12

2

Rubes and Rowdies

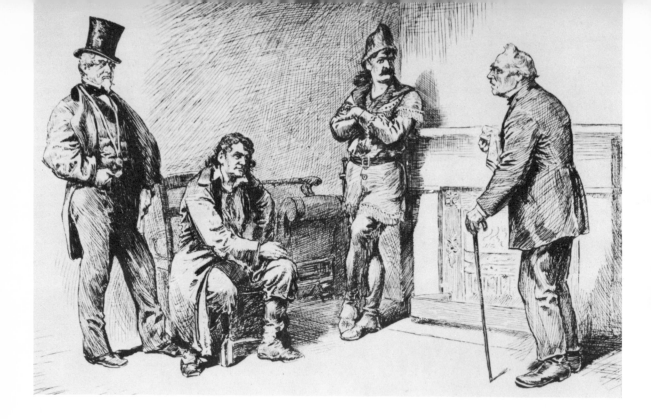

In the early American drama, you didn't have much future as a comedian if you couldn't play the part of a country rube or a city rowdy.

Theater audiences emitted early American "yaks" at the Yankee characters descended from the Jonathan of *The Contrast*. There was something very funny in homespun awkwardness combined with a cracker-barrel common sense and a disdain for fancy manners. We have laughed at modernday Jonathans such as a Will Rogers or a Fred Allen.

Tom Wignell's creation was to be the basis for a long line of Jonathans.

There was Jonathan Norrard of 1792, Jonathan Postfree of 1806, Jonathan from the play *Love and Friendship* of 1809, Jonathan from *The Buck Tails* of 1815, Jonathan Ploughboy in *The Forest Rose* of 1825, Jonathan in *A Trip to Niagara* of 1830, Jonathan in *The Patriot* and *Jonathan Dubikins,* both in 1834. In addition to the characters who carried forward the actual name of Jonathan, there were dozens and dozens of Yankee types based on the original Jonathan concept who took on other names such as Jedidiah Homebred, Deuteronomy Dutiful, Hiram Dodge, Solomon Swap, Nimrod Wildfire, Solon Shingle, etc.

Almost any actor of the period who aspired to prominence, especially in the field of comedy, was swept into a "Yankee" role — so popular was the demand. After Wignell there was James H. Hackett, first native American star; George H. (Yankee) Hill who followed in Hackett's footsteps; Joshua Silsbee; Dan Marble; John E. Owens, and countless others.

Typical of the period's humor was the following from the comedian "Yankee" Hill:

I once courted a gal by the name of Deb Hawkins. I made it up to get married. Well, while we was going up to the deacon's, I stepped my foot into a mud puddle, and spattered the mud all over Deb Hawkins' new gown, made out of her grandmother's old chintz petticoat. Well, when we got to the deacon's, he asked Deb if she would take me for her lawful wedded husband. "No," says she, "I shan't do no such thing." "What on airth is the reason?" says I. "Why," says she, "I've taken a mislikin' to you." Well, it was all up with me then, but I give her a string of beads, a few kisses, some other notions, and made it all up with her; so we went up to the deacon's a second time. I was determined to come up to her this time, so when the deacon asked me if I would take her for my lawfully wedded wife, says I, "No, I shan't do no such thing." "Why," says Deb, "what on airth is the matter?" "Why" says I, "I have taken a mislikin' to *you* now." Well, there it was all up again, but I gave her a new apron, and a few other little trinkets, and we went up again to get married. We expected then we would be tied so fast that all nature couldn't separate us, and when we asked the deacon if he wouldn't marry us, he said "No, I shan't dew any sich thing." "Why, what on airth is the reason?" says we. "Why," says he, "I've taken a mislikin' to both of you." Deb burst out crying, the deacon burst out scolding, and I burst out laughing.

At times so true to life were the impersonations that when Joshua Whitcomb, a Yankee character, was taken to Keene, New Hampshire, to present a play, the audi-

Many Yankee comedians chewed tobacco constantly and whittled sticks while on the stage. Pictured on the opposite page above are famous Yankee characters Bardwell Slote, Rip Van Winkle, Davy Crockett and Josh Whitcomb. Below are George H. (Yankee) Hill and Joshua Silsbee, Yankee impersonators of the period.

15

Typical scene of a comedy in an early American theater, Burton's in New York City.

ence wanted its money back. It couldn't understand being charged admission. Wasn't the character on the stage exactly the same as any number of local citizens who could be seen daily without charge?

Said a representative in protest, "It warn't no acting; it was jest a lot of fellers goin' around and doin' things."

The classic comedian, John E. Owens, is described as "one of the most comical men that have graced and cheered the stage." Owens was a comic actor who was naturally funny. He had a buoyant and merry temperament and great vitality. It is said comedy sparkled from his bright brown eyes. His role as Solon Shingle in a play *The People's Lawyer* was known throughout the country.

Shingle was an old Yankee farmer, described by the New York *Herald* as the type whom "everyone who has been in that vague place, 'the country,' must remember. He dresses shabbily, but carries fifty-dollar bills in his pocket; he makes absurd and ridiculous remarks, but yet has a fund of shrewd sense; he seems very simple and yet is not to be easily outwitted."

Crowds packed the theater nightly when Owens appeared, and quotations from the old farmer such as "Why, how do you do?" or "Jesso, jesso," were repeated

Playbills of John E. Owens and George H. (Yankee) Hill. Owens is shown portraying Solon Shingle, one of his most popular Yankee characters.

widely on the streets, in the horse cars and drawing rooms, by people who wished to appear witty. Acquaintances would greet each other on the street, "Why, Mr. Winslow, how-do-you-do?" and roar with laughter. In the mid-1800's Owens in *The People's Lawyer* achieved the longest run known till then in New York City or any city in America.

One newspaper, noting the fact that Owens had reached his hundredth performance of Solon Shingle, said:

In one hundred days France passed through the throes of two revolutions — lost a king, gained an emperor and again bowed to a king. In one hundred days Napoleon left Elba, marched to the throne of France, fought Waterloo, and was conquered.

In one hundred nights, John Owens fought a fight for popularity single-handed against the hordes of New York theater-goers, and conquered them. In one hundred nights the Broadway theater passed from the position of a concert hall to the height of fashion. We take pleasure in chronicling such great victories. *Solon Shingle* will run additional hundreds of nights if this great artist so chooses.

Scarcely less popular than the Yankee of the period was the character of Mose, the tough citizen of New York's Bowery.

Just as the comic-type Jonathans emerged from actual rural life of the times, so was a character to arise reflecting the situation in the big cities, especially New York.

The most depraved conditions existed in certain sections of New York City, especially that area called the Five Points located in the district bounded by Broadway, Canal Street, the Bowery and Park Row.

It was part of New York's Sixth Ward, sometimes known as the "Bloody Sixth." Reporting on his visit to this section, Charles Dickens, the novelist, said: "Here are lanes and alleys paved with mud knee-deep; underground chambers where they dance and game; . . . hideous tenements which take their names from robbery and murder; all that is loathsome, drooping and decayed is here."

It was from this congestion, poverty and misery forced upon newly arrived immigrants that was to spring one of the great comic characters of American theater history.

In 1849 before a clamorous audience at the old Olympic Theater in New York, the first presentation was given by Francis S. Chanfrau of *Mose, the Bow'ry B'hoy*. In this play and in *A Glance at New York*, which was presented in 1848, Chanfrau presented the rough-and-tumble, boisterous, comic type of performance for which he became famous.

As a boy Chanfrau lived in New York's Bowery and was himself one of the rough-and-ready youngsters that he portrayed on the stage. In presenting a play reflecting sordid aspects of city life, even though from a humorous point of view, Chanfrau was concerned that New Yorkers might resent seeing themselves realistically . . . soap locks, red shirt, plug hat, pants in boots, cigar-smoking corrupt politicians and all. The very first line of the play was a statement by Mose: "I'm bound not to run wid der machine any more."

But the response was enthusiastic. For the first time residents of the slums, the underprivileged of the Sixth Ward, began to frequent the theater to see entertain-

Entered according to Act of Congress in the Year 1848 by E&J Brown in the Clerks Office of the District Court of the Southern District of N.Y.

"I'M BOUND NOT TO RUN WID DER MACHINE ANY MORE."

F.S. CHANFRAU IN THE CHARACTER OF "MOSE"

As originally written for, and performed by him at the Olympic and Chatham Theatres, New York.

Lith & Published by E. & J. Brown 140 Fulton St N.Y.

TAKE OUT DE BUTT.

THE LAST SCENE IN BAKERS NEW PLAY OF "NEW-YORK AS IT IS", AS PERFORMED AT THE CHATHAM THEATRE.

A scene from one of F. S. Chanfrau's early "Mose" plays.

ment that reflected their own lives. The politicians came, too. So did the wealthy theatergoers.

True, the newsboys, butcher boys, Bowery B'hoys, and ward heelers did not always behave properly. Once the management at a Chanfrau production had to warn the pit where the cheap seats were located: "Boys, if you misbehave yourselves, I shall raise the prices." Women rarely sat in the pit, which was pervaded with foul smells. Not uncommonly, in the midst of a performance, rats ran out of holes in the floors into the orchestra.

The Mose series as presented by Chanfrau was filled with reflections of the big-city underworld and the constant battles between the gangs that frequented the Bowery. There was *Mose in California, Mose in a Muss, Mose's Visit to Philadelphia, Mose in China.* So popular did Chanfrau become that at one period he played Mose sketches in two New York theaters and one in Newark, New Jersey, on the same night.

But the Yankee and Mose comedians were not the only early American laugh makers. There were also the clowns. . . .

20

3

Clowns: White Face and Black

There was a time when the most popular American actors painted their faces and the most popular American actresses did not. Those days — along with the old-fashioned minstrel show, the circus and vaudeville — appear to be gone forever.

Two of the greatest clowns of America's early history were Dan Rice and George L. Fox. Rice achieved the height of his popularity in America shortly before the mid-1800's. He started his career aboard a showboat, going from port to port in the Midwest, clowning.

He was first engaged in 1840 in a traveling puppet show near Reading, Pennsylvania, where he used to exhibit a trained pig. To achieve his comic effects, Rice depended largely on his educated animals ranging from pigs to mules to horses.

His trick horse, Excelsior, could do and understand almost everything. The Dan Rice troupe, three performers, a band and Excelsior, traveled the land entertaining thousands of people. His admirers increased and Rice became known as "the most versatile, spectacular and beloved circus Jester of any country."

In New Orleans his fans erected a "Dan Rice Theater." When he took his circus to Washington he fraternized with such notables as Horace Greeley, Stephen A. Douglas and Robert E. Lee.

During the Civil War, Rice became a friend of President Lincoln and frequently visited him at the White House where the pair would swap humorous stories until far into the night.

Rice is said to have been one of Lincoln's main sources of funny anecdotes. It may have been vice versa. After the Civil War, Rice turned to politics, even seriously seeking the nomination for the Presidency against Grant in 1868. Although he received surprising support, he lost the nomination.

Perhaps even surpassing Rice in his accomplishments was George L. Fox, "one of the really funny men of his day." Fox was the first popular American entertainer to follow the ancient tradition of using white pigment on his face as the symbol of the clown.

Left:

Dan Rice, "King of American Clowns." He is the only famous comedian to run seriously for the United States Presidency.

Right:

George L. Fox, white-face clown and pantomimist. He performed for the troops during the Civil War.

Fox had amazing control of his facial muscles and was an expert in the comedian's art of "mugging." A critic of the period remarked that Fox was not content to please merely by being knocked down numerous times and jumping over tables and through windows. His muteness and passivity were infinitely more ludicrous than the bustling antics of other clowns, as also was his affectation of ignorant simplicity and credulous innocence.

At the old Olympic Theater on Broadway and Bleecker Street in New York, Fox's burlesque of Hamlet was a sure-fire laugh getter. Wrote Laurence Hutton, the critic:

He followed the text of Shakespeare closely enough to preserve the plot of the story, and never sank into imbecility or indelicacy . . .
To see Mr. Fox pacing the platform before the Castle of Elsinore protected against the eager and nipping air of the night by a fur cap and collar, and with mittens and arctic overshoes over the traditional costume of Hamlet; to see the woeful melancholy of his face as he spoke the most absurd of lines; to watch the horror expressed on his countenance when the Ghost appeared; to hear his familiar conversation with that Ghost, and his untraditional profanity when commanded by the Ghost to "swear" . . . was as thoroughly and ridiculously enjoyable as any piece of acting our stage has seen . . .

Fox burlesqued Hamlet for ten straight weeks. While this was tremendously successful it did not match his portrayal of the clown role of Humpty-Dumpty which he presented to the New York public alone more than twelve hundred times, a record for his period.

What Dan Rice and George L. Fox were to clowning, Thomas D. Rice was to the start of blackface minstrel comedy. Known as "Daddy" Rice, he achieved fame in entertainment circles almost overnight by blackening his face and doing a comic dance on the stage to the tune of the verse:

> "Wheel about, turnabout
> Do just so,
> And everytime I wheel about
> I jump Jim Crow!"

Rice was widely imitated. At that time, of course, the words Jim Crow had not taken on the symbolic meaning of racial prejudice which they have today. They were actually the name of an elderly Negro who did a dance similar to that which Rice popularized on the stage.

At the height of Rice's fame he induced the comedian, Joseph Jefferson II, to permit him to introduce his four-year-old son, Joseph Jefferson III, onto the stage. For this event, Rice used a bag which he carried over his shoulder. At the opportune moment he opened it and out stepped little Jefferson, also in blackface, who promptly went into a dance with Rice's six-foot figure towering alongside.

The act became the talk of the country. Rice himself attained unequaled popularity. The burnt cork and blackface which he originated have, of course, become a commonplace since.

24

AMERICAN THEATRE BOWERY NEW YORK

View of the Stage on the fifty seventh night of Mr. T. D. RICE of Kentucky in his original and celebrated extravaganza of JIM CROW on which occasion every department of the house was thronged to an excess unprecedented in the records of theatrical attraction — New York 25th. November 1833

Thomas D. "Daddy" Rice in his early success as a dancer. He helped originate the American minstrel show.

The minstrel show developed into America's sole "native" form of entertainment.

The advent of the American minstrel show dates from the 1830's and '40's with the innovations of "Daddy" Rice. The minstrel character had its roots in the days of slavery when Negroes were forced to dance and sing for their white masters. The adaptation into the minstrel show of the Negro songs and dances by northern white imitators became the sole branch of our dramatic art to have its beginnings in this country.

The influence of the minstrel extends in many ways to present-day comedy. The interlocutor of the minstrel show was really the father of the foil or "straight man" of vaudeville and of radio and television.

Popular as the minstrel became, he was destined to have a mature life of no more than twenty-five years before he surrendered the major entertainment spotlight.

These twenty-five years were destined to see the comic spirit move West with the advancing frontier.

4

Go West, Young Comedian!

There were many stories about the Wild West which might have discouraged an eastern actor from leaving home.

For example, John T. Raymond, the comedian, spread the report that "it is the duty of the door-keeper at a Western theater to collect the weapons of the audience before admitting the people to the house. . . . The bowie knife of a Texan critic never weighs less than fourteen pounds. . . ."

But there were compelling reasons why many actors went West.

Prosperity in the East was an uncertain quantity. Frequent economic crises threw many people out of work. The land to the westward gave promise of a freer, better life despite the hardships of frontier living.

Together with covered-wagon migrations went touring theatrical troupes. They came from Boston and New York on to Philadelphia, Charleston, Pittsburgh, St. Louis, Salt Lake City, New Orleans, San Francisco.

It was serious business, settling a new nation. Perhaps that was one reason why comedians were so welcome, even though the reception was often a rough one.

Whereas the sedate audiences that frequented the theater were mostly limited to well-to-do groups, the newly developing comedy tended to attract the rough-and-ready sections of the population who were not as concerned about manners as they were about having a thoroughly good time.

Mrs. Trollop, visiting writer from England, was shocked by the audiences which gathered in the new theaters:

Men came into the lower tier or boxes without their coats; and I have seen shirt-sleeves tucked to the shoulders; the spitting was incessant. . . .

The bearing and attitudes of the men is perfectly indescribable; the heels are higher than the head, the entire rear of the person presented to the audience . . . the noises, too, are perpetual, and of the most unpleasant kind; the applause is expressed by cries and thumping with the feet instead of clapping; and when a patriotic fit seizes them, and "Yankee Doodle" is called for, every man seems to think his reputation as a citizen depends on the noise he makes.

Among the young comedians who went West was Joseph Jefferson III, one of a long line of comedians who had appeared upon the stage as the youthful prodigy of "Daddy" Rice. Himself now a laugh maker of note, the young Jefferson headed west on a barnstorming trip to Chicago, then on to Springfield, Illinois.

When Jefferson and his company reached Springfield they discovered that a re-

Young Joseph Jefferson III at about the time he met attorney Abe Lincoln.

ligious revival was in progress and the fathers of the church not only launched forth against the theater in sermons but had taken political measures to have a new law passed, virtually outlawing by taxation theatrical presentations of any kind.

This created a difficult situation for the comedians and for the theater managers who had invested considerable sums in founding a theater in the city. Furthermore, the town was full of people at this time, and a guaranteed audience was on hand. But the interdict against performing was not a matter to be treated lightly. As Mr. Jefferson himself described it:

In the midst of our trouble a young lawyer called on the managers. He had heard of the injustice and offered, if they would place the matter in his hands, to have the license taken off, declaring that he only desired to see fair play, and he would accept no fee whether he failed or succeeded.

The case was brought up before the council. The young lawyer began his harangue. He handled the subject with tact, skill and humor, tracing the history of the drama from the time when Thespis acted in a cart to the stage of today. He illustrated his speech with a number of anecdotes, and kept the council in a roar of laughter; his good humor prevailed and the exorbitant tax was taken off.

This young lawyer was very popular in Springfield, and was honored and beloved by all who knew him, and after the time of which I write he held rather an important position in the government of the United States.

This was not to be the only occasion on which Abraham Lincoln expressed his interest in the subject of the theater. As President, Lincoln enjoyed comedy and comedians. In addition to his friendship with Jefferson and Dan Rice, Lincoln admired the famous actor James H. Hackett, one of the Yankee comedians who fol-

NIBLO'S GARDEN

LESSEE AND MANAGER.................WM. WHEATLEY
Stage Manager.........................Mr. L. J. Vincent
Musical Director.......................Mr. Harvey B. Dodworth
Scenic Artist..........................Mr. J. H. Selwyn

SECOND NIGHT
—OF—
MR. HACKETT

When, in consequence of the strongly expressed desire for its repetition, he will appear for
THE SECOND TIME IN HIS
WORLD-RENOWNED PERSONATION OF
FALSTAFF
SHAKESPEARE'S GREATEST COMIC CREATION.
MR. WM. WHEATLEY · as · PRINCE HAL

James H. Hackett in his role as *Falstaff* which attracted the commendation of President Lincoln. Hackett was one of the first native American theatrical stars and was a master of mimicry. Hackett's early reputation was gained from his "Yankee" roles.

Joseph Jefferson, in one of his most popular roles, that of Asa Trenchard in *Our American Cousin*.

lowed in the "Jonathan" tradition. By this time Hackett had become known for his role as Falstaff in various Shakespearean productions.

On one occasion after the President had attended a Hackett performance, the comedian sent to the White House a copy of his book, *Notes and Comments on Shakespeare*. The President acknowledged the gift, saying:

"Months ago I should have acknowledged the receipt of your book and accompanying kind note; and now I have to beg your pardon for not having done so. For one of my age I have seen very little of the drama. The first presentation of Falstaff I ever saw was yours here, last winter or spring. Perhaps the best compliment I can pay is to say, as I truly can, I am very anxious to see it again . . ."

Lincoln had come a long way from the time when, as a young lawyer, he had helped Joseph Jefferson win the right to present a play in Springfield. So had the young comedian.

Jefferson's rise had not been easy. Somehow many theater managers refused to recognize him as a comedian:

"Oh, you are the new young comedian, eh?" was the way one manager greeted me.

"Yes, sir," I replied, "there is no doubt about my being young; but how much of a comedian I am remains to be seen."

"Humph! Quite modest, too. Modesty is a good thing if it is not carried too far," he said. "Where have you been acting lately?"

I told him I had just finished starring in an engagement in Cumberland.

"Starring, oh! Then you are not so modest after all," he replied, "I suppose you have heard that my present comedian is a failure?"

I told him that the welcome news had reached me and as I had also been informed that in consequence of this the gentleman was about to retire from the amphitheater, I made bold to apply for the vacancy.

"Well," said Mr. Foster, "my funny man is certainly the most dismal piece of humanity I have ever met with. I engaged him on his face. I never saw such a comical outside belonging to such a serious inside. The man's mug is as funny as Liston's [comedian of the time] whom he resembles very much; large, round eyes, fat chops and turned up nose. I thought when I first saw him that, like the milkmaid, his face was his fortune; but no, as soon as he opens his mouth, all the humor seems to vanish. Now about yourself. I suppose you know . . . the actor has a great deal of hard work to do. It is what I call physical comedy; and you are too light for that business, I fancy."

I told him that I regretted this for if he engaged me by the pound my salary would perhaps be as light as myself.

"But you do not look like a comedian," he said to me. "You have a serious melancholy expression; you look more like an undertaker."

Jefferson's special talents as described by his friend William Winter included his ability "to touch, in his true and delicate manner, the springs of tears and laughter. . . ."

Jefferson's acting has always been remarkable for tenderness of heart . . . and for the spontaneous drollery, the condition of being an amusing person, which comes by nature, and which cannot be taught. . . . His crowning excellence as a comedian is, that he . . . does not stop at being a photographic copyist of the eccentric, the rustic, the ludicrous and the grotesque. . . . The level upon which he treads is that of humanity, in its laughable, mournful admixture of weakness, suffering, patience, amiability, despondency, hope and endeavor. . . .

Jefferson's first major comic role was that of Asa Trenchard in the play *Our American Cousin* which was presented for the first time in 1858. The play ran 140 consecutive nights.

It was, however, as Rip in the play *Rip Van Winkle* that Jefferson earned his great reputation. Seeing Jefferson perform, John Drew, the noted actor, exclaimed: "Gentlemen, I have had a very pleasant experience; I have seen a part played as well as it could be." Said another contemporary of Jefferson:

More than either of his ancestors, and more than most of his contemporaries, the present Jefferson is an originator in the art of acting. The comedians of past periods were rich in humor . . . but no name . . . has shone with a more tranquil lustre, or can be more confidently committed to the esteem of posterity.

De Wolf Hopper, himself a comedian, defined Jefferson as "the greatest comedian our stage has known . . . and the most self-effacing," while Henry Watterson, famed editor, said that Jefferson did more than anyone to "elevate the social and intellectual standing of the actor and the stage."

One incident relating to Jefferson and the death of a fellow comedian, George Holland, is revealing.

When Holland died, the family asked Jefferson to call upon the pastor of a near-by church and ask him to officiate at the service.

Jefferson went to the minister and explained that they wished to have arrangements made for the time and place of the funeral. As Jefferson himself describes it, he saw "an unmistakable change in the expression" in the minister's face when he learned that Mr. Holland had been an actor. At that point the minister refused pointblank to perform the funeral rites. Said Jefferson, recalling the incident:

I rose to leave the room with a mortification that I cannot remember to have felt before or since. I paused at the door and said:
"Well, sir, in this dilemma is there no other church to which you can direct me from which my friend can be buried?"
He replied that, "There is a little church around the corner" where I might get it done; to which I answered:
"Then God bless the little church around the corner," so I left the house.

The incident somehow got into the newspapers and brought a storm of protest. The fact that the Church of the Transfiguration (The Little Church Around the Corner) willingly accepted the funeral and Holland was buried in a quiet ceremony did not for a moment bury the incident itself.

On the contrary, it was picked up in the various newspapers and made the subject of front-page and nation-wide editorial discussion. *The New York Times* of December 29, 1870, said:

We may think what we please of any man's profession during his life but to follow him with resentment after death on account of it, to pronounce a decree that he is fit only for the bottomless pit, and that no word of the Redeemer's love or of the Resurrection should be pronounced over his grave — there is something so horrible in all this that we can scarcely believe it has really occurred in our own day and our own city.

34

THE HOLLAND TESTIMONIAL.

GRAND CONCERTED DEMONSTRATION
BY THE
DRAMATIC PROFESSION
FOR THE
BENEFIT OF THE WIDOW AND CHILDREN
OF THE
LATE GEORGE HOLLAND.
UNEXAMPLED PROGRAMME.

Through the hearty liberality of all the Managers, and the generous and prompt co-operation of the entire dramatic and musical professions, the Committee in charge of the Holland Testimonial have the privilege and pleasure of submitting to the public of New-York and Brooklyn the subjoined extraordinary combination of attractions.

TO BE SIMULTANEOUSLY PRESENTED
ON THURSDAY AFTERNOON, JAN. 19,
at Eleven different Theatres in New-York and
Brooklyn,
COMPRISING THE MOST BRILLIANT TALENT
IN THE COUNTRY.

NIBLO'S.

Lessees and Managers,
Messrs. JARRETT & PALMER.
To commence at 1¼ P. M.

PERFECTION.	Mr. GEO. RYER, Mr. H.
SAN FRANCISCO MIN-	R. TEESDALE, (his first
STRELS.	appearance in America,)
SONG......Miss FANNY	Mr. FRED'K DEWAR,
PRESTIGE.	(his first appearance in
DANIEL IN THE	America,) Mr. A. FITZ-
BRYANT'S DEN.	GERALD, Mr. T. HAM-
DAN BRYANT,	ILTON, Mr. B. MAGIN-
NELSE SEYMOUR,	LEY, Mr. C. H. MOR-
LITTLE MAC.	TON, Mr. F. ROGERS,
RECITATION,	Mr. J. FRANKLIN, Mr.
Mr. GEO. VANDEN-	J. ROBERTSON, Mr. E.
HOFF.	K. COLLIER, Mr. R.
(as also at Wallack's and	SMITH, Mr. F. CLARKE,
Fifth-avenue Theatre on	Miss PAULINE MARK-
the same day.)	HAM, Miss FANNY
THE BLACK CROOK	PRESTIGE, Miss RAW-
BALL-ROOM SCENE.	LINSON.
MISS LYDIA THOMP-	Mrs. WRIGHT,
SON	BONFANTI,
and	ALL THE PREMIERES,
Mr. HARRY BECKETT,	THE GRAND BALLET,
in scene from	THE MAJILTONS,
PARIS,	Messrs. MOE
(by permission of Mr.	and
Henderson.)	GOODRICH.

BOOTH'S THEATRE.

Proprietor and Manager........Mr. EDWIN BOOTH
To commence at 1 P. M.

	Mr. EDWIN BOOTH, Mr.
Shakespeare's Comedy of	LAWRENCE P. BAR-
	RETT, Mr. W. E. SHER-
	IDAN, Mr. A. W. FEN-
KATHARINE ANE PE-	NO, Mr. D. C. ANDER-
	SON, Mr. AUG. PITOU,
TRUCHIO.	Mr. R. PATEMAN, Mr. J.
	HOWSON, Master SEY-
and	MOUR, Mr. N. DECKER,
	Mr. HOGAN, Mrs. SEY-
	MOUR, F. INTREPIDI,
W. J. Robson's	A. JACQUES, F. C.
	RICHARDSON, C. RO-
	SINE, C. J. DADE, F. F.
LOVE AND LOYALTY.	BRENNAN, J. TAYLOR,
	Miss PATEMAN, Miss
	LIVINGSTON.

FIFTH-AVENUE THEATRE.

Sole Lessee and Manager....Mr. AUGUSTIN DALY
Commences at 1 P. M.
RECITATION.

Mr. G. VANDENHOFF,

1½ P. M.,

and also at Wallack's and
Niblo's same day.

Mr. Bronson C. Howard's
Comedy,

SARATOGA.

RECITATION.

Miss AGNES ETHEL.

FANNY MORANT, Miss
LINDA DIETZ, Mrs.
GILBERT, Mrs. WIN-
TER, Miss AMES, Misses
CLAXTON, VOLMER,
NORWOOD, KEENE.

OLYMPIC.

Commences at 2 P. M.
Lessee and Manager............Mr. JAS. E HAYES
L. FOX, Mr.
Mr. W.
Miss

CROSBY'S OPERA HOUSE.

GRAND TESTIMONIAL

TO BE GIVEN TO THE

'Little Church Round the Corner,'

Thursday Afternoon, Feb. 16, at 2:30,

Under the direction of

Jos. F. Wheelock, J. W. Blaisdell, John W. Jennings, and Owen Fawcett.

Treasurer:.................................G. W. GARRISON

The Opera House has been kindly tendered by Mr. ALBERT CROSBY.

The following papers have given the gratuitous use of their columns, viz.: Chicago Times, Chicago Tribune, Republican, Eve......ning Mail, and the Evening Journal.

Order of performan.....

1. Overture..............
2. "Little Church R......
C. S. Frederi......
tram, J. J......
Leader..............
3. Prof. Hazelmay......
4. "Let Me Like a......
Leader..............
5. Tragic revival......
6. Clodoche danc......
Mess......
7. Eugene (a la F......
Yet so Fer......
8. Song and da......
9.............
Lawyer J. He......
Sheepface......
Old Snarl......
Judge Banni......

THE HOLLAND TESTIMONIAL.

Twelve Matinees for a Charity.

No one can now regret the form chosen for the opening performances in aid of the Holland Testimonial Fund. It was feared that the division of interest arising from giving a dozen different entertainments, in as many different places, would lessen the aggregate results. If all people who contributed might be enabled to see each other, as it were, in the act of doing so, it was thought the attendance would be more numerous. This has not proved, so far, to be the case. The public is more generous and self-abnegatory than it had credit for being. Some of the houses, yesterday afternoon, were very fine indeed, and all, numerically speaking, were respectable. The feeling shown by the audiences was universally quite delightful to see. Every allusion to the occasion of all these gatherings was received with the utmost enthusiasm. Whatever misgivings any of the Committee may have originally felt as regards the prudence of giving all these performances simultaneously, were certainly altogeth......

Where......
it seems......
may, b......
south, s......
was qu......
receive......
M......

The Out-of-Town Contributions to the Fund—"The Little Church Around the Corner" Remembered.

BALTIMORE, Md., Jan. 19.—The receipts of a matinée given this afternoon, at the Holiday-street Theatre, for the Holland Testimonial Fund, were $500, all of which will be forwarded to New-York, the manager, Mr. Ford, having personally assumed all incidental expenses. In addition to JOHN S. CLARKE and the regular dramatic company of the theatre, all principal artistes of the English Opera Company, except Mrs. CAROLINE RICHINGS BERNARD, who was absent, on account of the death of her father PETER RICHINGS, volunteered and appeared. The audience was large and fashionable.

VICKSBURG, Jan. 19.—The Opera-house gave a matinée this afternoon, in response to the call for the Holland testimonial. The gross receipts go to the "Little Church around the Corner."

Some of the comments and newspaper reports from Chicago, Baltimore and New York indicating the degree of interest in the "Little Church Around the Corner" incident.

The stained-glass memorial window at the "Little Church Around the Corner" which depicts Joseph Jefferson carrying the shrouded figure of George Holland. Jefferson and Holland are the only American comedians to be so enshrined.

Nor did the incident stop with the critical comment of the press. On January 19, 1871, every New York theater opened its doors for a benefit for the Holland family. Actors, singers, acrobats, dancers, comedians volunteered their services as a loving testimony.

There were similar testimonials in support of The Little Church Around the Corner and for the benefit of Holland's widow and children in Brooklyn, San Francisco, Boston, Vicksburg, Washington, D. C., and elsewhere.

In Chicago, as reported in the Chicago *Tribune*:

Chicago has witnessed a great many crowds in places of public entertainment but nothing to compare with that of yesterday, the hour and the day of the benefit for Holland. . . . When it became evident that the house could not even possibly hold those who had purchased tickets, the box office was closed thus leaving a crowd who must turn in an attempt to go back. The result was that for a long time it made a perfect blockade, neither party being able to make any progress. The scene around the box office became very exciting. Men held up their money in the air and offered ten, twenty, twenty-five, fifty and even as high as seventy-five dollars to the doorkeeper to let them go through.

The burial of George Holland actually marked more than the passing of a comedian. It marked the end of an era. While Jefferson himself lived on to continue his portrayal of Rip Van Winkle and even to participate in an early motion picture, the times were changing.

A new type of comedian was in the wings of the American theater eager to take the spotlight. He was not to be in the image of a Holland or a Jefferson. Rather he was to revert back to a Chanfrau or a crude type of Jonathan. Music-hall and vaudeville comedy was about to be born and Tony Pastor was the father.

36

5

Low Comedy and the Elegant Eighties

THE NEW YORK MIRROR

A REFLEX OF THE DRAMATIC EVENTS OF THE WEEK.

NEW YORK: SATURDAY, JANUARY 4, 1879.   Price Five Ce[nts]

No. 12 Union Square.   *VOL. I. #1*

STANDARD THEATRE, Broadway and 33d St.
WM. HENDERSO[N], Proprietor and Manager.
LAST WEEK.
LAST NIGHT[S] of the Great Play of
Farewell Perform[ance] Season.
ALM[OST] A LIFE.
Farewell Mati[nee], Saturday, 1:30 P.M.,
Saturday Evening, January 4, sixty-third and
last night o[f] G[rand], January 6, Miss Katy
MONDAY EVENI[NGS], supported by the Stan-
MAYHEW, in M'Liny. dard Theatre Comedy Company.
POPULAR PRICES.

BOOTH'S THEATRE.
MANAGER, N December 30.
Monday[s] WEEK.
[L]A combination in a
Stetson['S] A DOUBLE BILL.
GRAND GA[LA] and incidents of two Bur-
lesques; extreme[ly] ANGELINE
EV[E] and
BABE[S] IN THE WOOD.
Hour[s] of Fun and Song.
Three Ho[urs] SONGS and RECITATIONS
GUS WILLIAMS [as] the Dancing Master in
JAMES MAFFI BABES. okey.
The Educated D[on]cing Heifer.
The Da[y] The Whales.
The Balloon Trip.
ENTIRE GREA[T] CLAR PRICES MAINTAINED
LESQUES. POP[ULAR] 50 cents.   25 cents.
25 cents; for children 25 cents.
Matine[es]

PARK THE[ATRE], OPERA BURLESQUE.
HENRY E. AB[BEY], Lessee and Manager.
[ITS] BEY. TIVE SUCCESS.
POP[ULAR] engagement of the famous
COLVILLE OPE[RA] BURLESQUE COMPANY.
W[ho] will appe[ar] at 8 o'clock, over at 10.30,
mencing prompt[ly] the Charming
B[ABES] IN THE WOOD.
BABE[S] Wealth of Attraction.
With all th[e] other Musical Selections, Bril-
Mlle. Rosean, in [char]acters, Handsome Costumes,
in it Cast of Che[nery], The Educated Donkey
an[d] Beautiful Seal episode N,
ox, ever seen [be]ore.
WHO KIL[LED] COCK ROBIN?
[Ch]ildren half [price] during this engagement.

NIBLO'S G[ARDEN] THEATRE.
[Mr.] STARIN, Prop'r and Manager.
Edward [D]AY, DEC. 30th, 1878.
MON[DAY] GREAT HOLIDAY ATTRACTION, for
E[very] Week G[ala] with Scenery, Costumes and
Ef[fe]cts on a [su]perproductions, and the grand-
e[st] thing in [the] city. Edward Falconer's
Greatfish D[.] PEEP O' DAY
[ni]gh[t]. MR. FRANK O'ANS,
Capt. Peep O['Da]y an extraordinary cast.
supporte[d]

BROADWAY THEATRE, Cor. 34th Street.
EDGAR & F[U]LTON, Lessees and Managers.
[LA]ST [NI]GHT MACAULEY. UNCLE DAN'L
[LA]ST NIGHT[S] MACAULEY. UNCLE DAN'L
[E]N[I]G, [JAS] MACAULEY. UNCLE DAN'L
RISE [S]EATS, 50c., 75c., and $1.
[MATI]NEE, SATURDAY.

C[.] [THEATRE]
[.] Broadway, opp. N.Y. Hotel.
F[ARS]. [.] Manager.
[A] FARMER'S DAUGHTER
[Gr]eat Hit of the Season.
[Endorsed] by the Press and Public
To [b]e a Grand Success.
[Or]chestra Chairs, 50 cents. Ad-
[mi]ssion, 25 cents.
S[TEINWAY] HALL, HERMAN LINDE
[Comm]encing JANUARY 6, 1879.
HE[R]MAN LINDE,
in a series of S[h]akespearean impersonations,
reciting fr[om] memory complete plays.
[In]itial work will be
"MACBETH."
"A towering [gi]ant in force among a com-
pany of F[ried]s deserves a crowded house.
"Herman Lin[de's] him Als.—Macbeth" I
as Macbeth, at his retentive-
[Be]sieged to with [it] with great interest. He
ness of memory[,] voice and great tragic
[po]wers. W[.] interpretation of immor[tal]

GERMANIA THEATRE,
AD. NEUENDORFF, Director.
Performance Every Evening at 8.
Box Office open from 8 a.m. to 10 p.m.

THEATRE COMIQUE, 514 Broadway.
HARRIGAN & HART, Proprietors.
Last Week of Ed. Harrigan's Original Play,
CHRISTMAS JOYS
AND
SORROWS.
HARRIGAN and HART,
will appear in two of their irresistible charac-
ters. Let no one fail to see the DARKEY WAKE.

BOWERY THEATRE,
FERDINAND W. HOFELE, Manager.

SAM DEVERE
as
JASPER.
Matinee Saturday at 2.

VOLK'S GARDEN, 199 Bowery, 201
—Opposite Spring Street—
LONDON MUSIC HALL OF AMERICA.
OPEN ALL THE YEAR AROUND.

MRS. PAUL FALK......PROPRIETRESS
WM. T. GEISELBERG.........MANAGER
GEORGE T. SHAW...STAGE MANAGER

STRICTLY FIRST-CLASS Variety talent
in all branches. None others accepted after
first night. Business must be sent in a few
days in advance. All aerial artists must
have a net.

FIFTH AVENUE THEATRE, 1915
JOSEPH JEFFERSON
as
RIP VAN WINKLE
Every night and Saturday Matinee.

TONY PASTOR'S,
The
BEST COMPANY IN THE WORLD
In a
GRAND HOLIDAY BILL
OF NOVELTIES.
THE KERNELS,
FRENCH TWIN SISTERS,
NILES AND EVANS,
etc., etc., etc.
Matinees Tuesday and Saturday.

MISS LAURA DON,
Mme. Laurent,
In "Only a Farmer's Daught[er]"
Globe Theatre.
Address at Mir[ror Office]

HARRY MEREDITH,
SEASON 1878-79.

WALNUT STREET THEATRE.

LESLIE GOSSIN,
as
Harold Lennox,
in
"Only a Farmer's Daughte[r]"
Wall's Dramatic [Co.]
Unio[n]
Address at MIRROR Office.

MISS CONSTANCE BA[.]
As Gretchen,
In "Rip Van Wi[nkle]"
Fifth Aven[ue]
Address at MIRROR Office.

WILLIAM GILL,
Comedian and St[.]
Colville Opera Burlesque Co[.]
Address as Mir[ror]

E. K. COLLIER,
COLLIER'S "CELEBRATED [.]
Address care MIRROR Office.

FRANK W. SANGER,
JUVENILES,
SEASON OF 1878-[9]
PARK TH[EATRE]

HARRY LEE,
LEADING JUVENILE M[AN]
CHESTNUT STREET [.]

CHARLES J. EDMONDS,
Principal Support of
Katie Mayhew.

MISS ADELAIDE CHER[.]
Address, 35 East Fourteen[th]

MISS LILLIAN CLEVES G[.]
Address,
Glenham Hot[el]

I. DAVEAU,
Broadway Theatre,
For th[e]

MISS MARIE CLARA HAST[.]
Leading Lady,
With Boniface's "Soldier's Tr[.]"
Address at Mirr[or]

EDWARD CHAPMAN,
Comedian,
With Jane Coombs, Octo[.]
Address at Mi[rror]

E. MURRAY DAY,
Leading Heavies or Fir[st]
Address

AMOS ELLSWORTH,
Boy Magician and Prestid[igitateur]
At Liberty. Address,
Brown & Pa[.] 804 Br[.]

FRANK M. CHAPMAN,
Agent and Business Ma[nager]
Fanny Davenp[ort]

MISS MARIE PRESCO[TT]
California Theatre, San [.]
Address at [.]

W. H. CROMPTON,
Stage Manager,
Season of 1878-79.
Broadway Thea[tre]

MISS STELLA CONGDON,
With Fanny Davenport,
Specially engaged as Baliech, in [.]

JAMES L. CARHART,
Address,
8th [.]

TONY PASTOR.

HARRY BLANCHARD,
Juvenile,
At Liberty. Address care of
E. B. Duffield,
12 Union Square.

ARCHIE BOYD,
As Higgins the Butler, in "Only a Farmer's Daughter."

HARRY GWYNETTE,
In "Chilperic" at Howard Atheneum,
Boston, Mass.
Address at Mirror Office.

EVA BYRON,
In "Chilperic" at Howard Atheneum,
Boston, Mass.
Address at Mirror Office.

THE LONDON, 285 and 287 Bowery, N.Y.
—Opposit[e] Prince St.—
THEATRE OPEN AL[L]

"You call yourself a comedian," a friend of Joseph Jefferson said to him on one occasion, "Why, you can only play one part. You are the prince of dramatic carpetbaggers and carry all your wardrobe in a gripsack. Look at that huge pile of trunks — mine, sir! mine! Examine my list of parts! Count them — half a hundred, at the very least. You ought to be ashamed of yourself. Where is your versatility?"

"My dear Charlie," said Jefferson, "you are confounding wardrobe with talent. What is the value of a long bill of fare if the stuff is badly cooked? You change your hat and fancy you are playing another character. Believe it, it requires more skill to act one part fifty different ways than to act fifty parts all the same way."

Although Jefferson's reply was witty it was not an answer to the changing time. The country was changing, its audiences were changing, and the comedy needs were changing, too.

The new comedy was no longer to be found in the theater of Jefferson and Hackett, popular as it remained. The music halls, the beer halls, the minstrel shows and burlesque were to be the cradle of the future comedy, and were to bring forth a new comedy theater — the variety or vaudeville show.

Before the Civil War, a young man by the name of Tony Pastor found employment in the circus, became a clown, tumbled with the acrobats and danced in the minstrel shows. In 1860 he became a comic vocalist in a Broadway music hall and then opened up his own place, a honky-tonk, offering beer, wine, liquor and hostesses.

Perhaps Tony Pastor had an instinct for recognizing entertainment talent. He conceived the idea of organizing a road show with plenty of comedy in it. It was a success from the outset. He increased his tours and played every prominent town on the map. In 1881 Pastor opened his 14th Street Theater in the Tammany Hall Building in New York. It was something new in clean entertainment. A "variety show": something for everyone. It was entertainment, somebody said, children could take their parents to. Under Tony's tutelage, many a future headliner learned the beginnings of the acting profession, especially comedy.

While Pastor was planting the seeds of future vaudeville, a man by the name of Michael B. Leavitt was doing the same for burlesque. Leavitt was a hard-headed and unsentimental gentleman, former child actor and manager of a troupe of minstrel and variety performers in the early days. It was Leavitt who brought into prominence a group of female minstrels in 1879 operating on both the East and West coasts, and who developed a variety form of entertainment which became the burlesque of modern times. To the names of Pastor and Leavitt was to be added a third, Benjamin Franklin Keith, to whom credit goes for founding modern circuit vaudeville. Having received his start in a dime museum as a circus man, Keith in 1883 broke with his partner, Batchelder, and bought the Bijou Theater in Boston where his ingenuity helped to invent the modern form of vaudeville.

Keith had the idea that a continuous show of entertainment would attract people. So one Sunday morning, he placed an advertisement in the Boston newspapers to advertise the continuous performance idea which stated: "Come when you please, stay as long as you like." The idea was revolutionary; but it worked. Admission

RULES AND REGULATIONS

WALLACK'S THEATRE.

...

1. Gentlemen, at the time of rehearsal of performance, are not to wear their hats in the Green Room, or talk vociferously. The Green Room is a place appropriated for the quiet and regular meeting of the company, who are to be called thence, *and thence only*, by the call boy, to attend on the stage. The Manager is not to be applied to in that place, on any matter of business, or with any personal complaint. For a breach of any part of this article, fifty cents will be forfeited.

2. The call for all rehearsals will be put up by the Prompter between the play and farce, or earlier, on evenings of performance. No plea that such call was not seen will be received. All rehearsals must be attended. For absence from each scene, a fine of twenty-five cents; whole rehearsal, five dollars.

3. Any person appearing intoxicated on the stage shall forfeit a week's salary, and be liable to be discharged.

4. For making stage wait—fine, one dollar.

5. A Performer rehearsing from a book or part at the last rehearsal of a new piece, and after proper time given for study, forfeits one dollar.

6. A Performer introducing his own language or improper jests not in the author, or swearing in his part, shall forfeit one dollar.

7. A Performer refusing a part allotted him or her, by the Manager, will forfeit his or her salary during the run of the piece, and on any night of its representation during the season, and be liable to be discharged by the Manager.

8. A Performer restoring what is cut out by the Manager, will forfeit one dollar.

9. A Performer absenting himself from the Theatre of an evening, when concerned in the business of the stage, will forfeit a week's salary, and be liable to be discharged by the Manager.

10. In all cases of sickness, the Manager reserves to himself the right of payment or stoppage of salary during the absence of the sick person.

11. No person permitted *on any account to address the audience*, without the consent of the Manager. *Any violation of this article will subject the party to forfeiture of a week's salary, and a discharge by the Manager.*

12. No *Prompter, Performer, or Musician* will be permitted to copy any manuscript or music belonging to the Theatre, without permission from the Manager, under the penalty of fifty dollars.

13. Every gentleman engaged in the Theatre is to provide himself with such silk or cotton tights and stockings, wigs, feathers, swords, shoes and boots as may be appropriate and necessary to the costume he is wearing. If the costume be of the present period, *the whole of it* must be provided by the Performer.

14. The regulations guiding the evening performances will apply equally to those given as matinees.

15. Ladies bringing servants, must on no account permit them behind the scenes.

16. Ladies and gentlemen are requested not to bring children behind the scenes, unless actually required in the business.

17. It is particularly requested that every lady and gentleman will report to the Prompter their respective places of residence.

18. Ladies and gentlemen prevented attending the rehearsal by indisposition will please give notice to the Prompter *before* the hour of beginning.

19. No stranger, or person not connected with the Theatre, will be admitted behind the scenes, without the written permission of the Manager.

20. Any new rule which may be found necessary shall be considered as part of these Rules and Regulations, after it is publicly made known in the Green Room.

Rules and regulations of the famous Wallack's Theatre of the later 1800's were hard on comedians. Ad libbing was penalized, as point six indicates.

was a dime in Boston's Bijou, and "for five cents more one could obtain a chair."

Some of his friends thought that he was heading for certain trouble if people could stay as long as they liked because the turnover, they feared, would be astonishingly small. Of course, P. T. Barnum, the circus king, had pretty much the same problem and he had solved it by putting up a sign which read THIS WAY TO THE EGRESS. Many of his customers thought that this was some kind of strange animal or bird and, upon walking through the door, found themselves out on the street.

Keith's variety or vaudeville show, as it came to be known, attracted greater and greater attention. The idea was extended from Boston to Providence to Philadelphia and eventually to New York where Keith took over the Union Square Theater which was then the home of the legitimate stage. Keith teamed up with B. F. Albee, and the Keith-Albee enterprises spread their influence throughout the developing nation.

Mrs. Keith was personally interested in her husband's enterprises, particularly from the point of view of removing the stigma of doubtful morality which surrounded the variety shows and music-hall entertainment. As the Keith Circuit grew, every theater carried a sign on its bulletin board backstage:

Notice to Performers

Don't say "slob" or "son of gun" or "Holy gee" on the stage unless you want to be cancelled peremptorily. Do not address anyone in the audience in any manner. If you have not the ability to entertain Mr. Keith's audiences without risk of offending them, do the best you can. Lack of talent will be less open to censure than would be an insult to a patron. If you are in doubt as to the character of your act, consult the local manager before you go on the stage, for if you are guilty of uttering anything sacrilegious or even suggestive, you will be immediately closed and will never again be allowed in a theater where Mr. Keith is in authority.

The years from 1877 to 1882 marked the end of the era of the great local stock companies and the start of an era of traveling companies. Shakespeare and the traditional repertoire were fading into the background. Musical comedy was taking the public by storm. New names, particularly the names of comedians, were coming into the popular tongue.

Most of the early variety comedy was racial or national, reflecting migration waves which brought Irish, Italian and Jewish people to these shores in large numbers. Comedy was crude and of doubtful humor by today's standards, but your grandfather or perhaps your great grandfather probably laughed at such side splitters as these:

Lotta Crabtree was a fabulous figure of the early American stage. One of the few comediennes with a national following, Lotta — as she was generally known — started on the West Coast as a red-headed child actress who could dance, sing and play the banjo. She developed into a national favorite and died the richest actress in America. Lotta is the only known comedienne in the nation's history whose memory is marked by a public fountain. "Lotta's Fountain" — donated by the wealthy actress to the city of San Francisco in 1875 — is located at the intersection of Kearny, Market and Geary Streets.

Straight Man: If I didn't have this hang-out here I don't know what I'd do. *(Inevitable knock)* Come in. *(Enter comic)*

Comic *(exaggerated Negro dialect):* Good mawnin'. I just stopped in for some information.

Straight: I'll try to accommodate you. What is it?

Comic: What time does the three o'clock train go out?

Straight: The three o'clock train? Why, it goes out exactly sixty minutes past two o'clock.

Comic: That's funny. The man at the station told me it went out exactly sixty minutes before four o'clock.

Straight: Well, you won't miss your train, anyway.

Comic: No. Well, I'm much obliged. *(Exits)*

Straight: Curious sort of chap. *(Picks up banjo and strums quietly as comic re-enters.)*

Comic: Excuse me, which is the other side of the street?

Straight: Why, the other side of the street is just across the way.

Comic: That's funny. I asked the fellow across the street and he said it was over here.

Straight: Well, you can't depend on everything you hear.

Comic: No, that's so.

At about this period one of the most celebrated teams in the history of the American theater became a New York sensation. It was the team of Edward Harrigan and Tony Hart, whose popularity knew no equal. The pair's shrewd realism and sympathetic understanding of racial and national values brought them a vast following.

Harrigan's plays had their inception as vaudeville sketches consisting of songs and dialogue. Out of these grew his full-length plays centering about the New York Irish. For fourteen years Harrigan and Hart were a much-esteemed and enormously successful team. To many out-of-towners Harrigan and Hart were a New York landmark equal in stature to Broadway. "A visit to New York would be as incomplete to the countryman if he did not see Harrigan and Hart, as if he had by some strange mistake missed going to Central Park," declared one New England guidebook in the eighties.

Edward Harrigan and Tony Hart in costume. Hart frequently played the role of a woman.

Harrigan and Hart complemented each other or as the Boston *Traveler* stated, "Hart could play all the parts seven Harrigans could write and Harrigan could write what seven Harts could play." Harrigan was a prolific writer. In addition to some eighty or ninety sketches that he wrote while working in variety theaters as a young actor, he was the author of some thirty-five full-length plays. Not only this, but Harrigan went on to act in his own plays, sing his own songs and finally ended up by producing, financing and directing them himself. He even wrote the text for his own programs.

Harrigan was sometimes characterized as "the Dickens of America." The appeal of the pair was not so much to the upper-class theatergoers of New York, but to the habitués of the slums, the newsboys, flowergirls, the barbers, the butchers, the Bowery toughs and the South Street sailors, the disreputable folks who had made up the bulk of the followers of Chanfrau and his Bowery-B'hoy productions of years before. Harrigan and Hart also attracted the politicians of New York, even though the team would engage in the sharpest satire against corrupt practices of the day. The gossipy weekly, *Town Topics,* reported in 1886 after attending a performance of the *O'Reagans*:

A brutal alderman sat beside me and roared when Mr. Wild (Harrigan) remarked with all his power that the politicians had stolen all the stars from the American flag and were now wearing the stripes. The brutal alderman did not believe him, of course, but it might be that if anyone in life had passed this same jest to him, he would probably have committed homicide or mayhem. This is the soul of Harrigan's peculiar talent. He sees the life he is a part of and translates it as a commentator, rather than as a critic.

For some twenty years Harrigan and Hart held sway over the New York theater. Their plays included the popular *Mulligan Guards* series which went to eight different sequels.

On one occasion when Harrigan and Hart threatened to separate such a hue and cry was raised that a special committee of politicians called upon New York's mayor, William R. Grace, and asked him as a civic contribution to offer his good services in an attempt to heal the breach. The Mayor dutifully tried and got nowhere. After the rift, both actors went their own ways but neither was able to achieve anything approaching their previous accomplishments. The influence of Harrigan and Hart carries through to this day.

The comedy team which followed closely upon their heels, McIntyre and Heath, owed much to the pioneering work of Harrigan and Hart. Jim McIntyre and Tom Heath were the Amos 'n' Andy of long ago. They started in 1874 and continued until the 1930's. The team is considered by many to be the greatest of all blackface acts. McIntyre and Heath were no slapstick comedians, but presented fine characterizations and drew real belly laughs. They became the oldest two-man act in vaudeville. Strangely enough, while the team maintained itself intact until the thirties, offstage the men seldom spoke to each other and even lived in different hotels when possible.

McIntyre and Heath took the full cycle of available mediums, variety, vaudeville, minstrel show, and even took part in a Broadway play, *The Hamtree;* but they al-

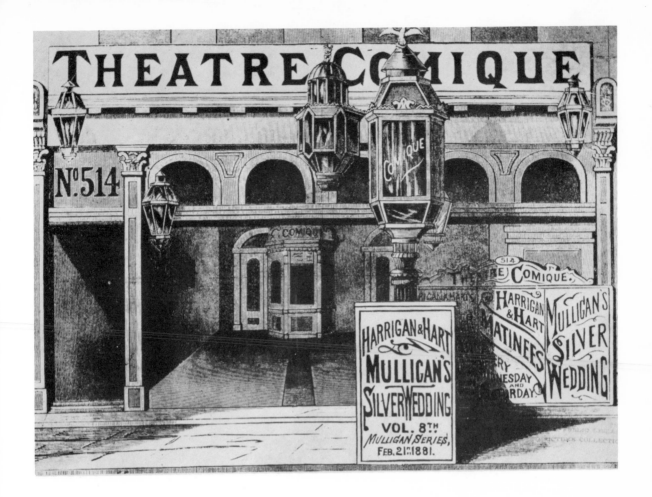

Harrigan and Hart's "Theatre Comique" on Broadway, New York City.

Harrigan and Hart comprised the most famous comedy team of their day. They continued the rough-and-tumble type of humor begun by Chanfrau many years before. A visit to New York was incomplete until you had seen a Harrigan and Hart Show.

ways returned to their first love, vaudeville. Tom Heath was the straight man while Jim McIntyre played the comic. Other best-known plays were *Red Pepper* and *The Georgia Minstrels.*

Joe Laurie, Jr., in his *Show Biz,* has this recollection of Tom Heath:

I'll never forget the time Tom Heath and I were sitting in the lobby of the Hollis Chambers in Boston looking out the big front windows (hotels those days had big store windows and the salesmen and actors would sit there and give the local girls the eye).

Tom was a tobacco chewer, and my foot was near the big brass cuspidor. I was afraid to pull my foot away for fear he would think I was underestimating his aim. (Remember, I was a kid and he was a big star.)

He certainly had me nervous for an hour but he proved just as big a star at spittin' tobacco juice as he was on the stage; he never missed the cuspidor once.

Jimmy McIntyre always assumed the role of the smaller and downtrodden colored man and Tom Heath was the overbumptious "Hennery." On the stage, McIntyre and Heath were so sure of each other that if one sprang a new joke, he knew that the other would come right back quick as a flash with a funny answer. People who had seen them do the same scene two nights in succession noted that the two versions might be entirely different.

"In all comedy teams," stated McIntyre, "there are the straight actor and the comedian. The former feeds the lines to the comedian so the latter can get off the jokes that bring the laughs. We have never worked that way. Heath is the straight man and I am the comedian. But the way we do things is this: Heath says something that gives me a chance to make a joke that gets a laugh; but my joke always gives him a chance to come back with an answer that gets another laugh."

"You might say that we're selling laughs," stated Heath. "If Jim can sell an extra one, I get half the proceeds. If I can sell an extra one, Jim gets half the proceeds. We never forget that we are financially interested in each other's work. That's the way men in any kind of business ought to feel."

Thomas McIntyre and James Heath were another successful blackface team. They worked together for over fifty years. When McIntyre died in 1937 he was followed to the grave one year later by his partner.

May Irwin, known as "Madam Laughter," had few equals as a comedienne on the legitimate stage in the 1880's. She lived long enough to be kissed in one of the first moving picture films made in this country.

Top women comedians were rare in the theater of the 1880's as they are today. But there was no more lovable comic character in the country than May Irwin, a product of Tony Pastor's variety shows, probably the most beloved woman of her period.

Much later, President Woodrow Wilson, who always enjoyed the theater, particularly May Irwin's comedy roles, once offered her "the portfolio of Secretary of Laughter." *Theatre Magazine* described Miss Irwin as "the funniest stage woman in America" and in an interview asked her how she got that way. Answered Miss Irwin:

Humor is spontaneous. It is born with one or it is not. It cannot be acquired and it cannot be forced. To illustrate: I often receive letters from magazines asking me to write on the humorous side of this or that. Many times I sit, my fountain pen clutched in my hand, my features tense as a tragedian's and nothing happens.

I have to write the editor: "I can't, that's all." Sometimes it is quite otherwise. The subject happens to come within the scope of my observations, it is comprised in the radius of my interests.

The other day an editor wrote me to write about the funny things I have seen on street-cars. I wrote it at once because it was something I had noticed and it was a favorite subject of mine.

Notice the next time you get on a streetcar the worried look of the men and women, the jaws thrust out, the foreheads gathered into hard knots, the lips down-drooping, the eyes hard and sullen. If there is one pleasant face, one good-natured looking person on the car, your eyes wander back again and again to look at him. . . .

To me humor is unanalyzable. It comes or it does not. It is as mysterious as and less controllable than electricity. That which is called the comic mind seizes upon the funny points in a play and makes the most of them.

In discussing her audiences, May Irwin told a friend, "I'm honest with my audiences. I never fool them. When my play goes on the road I go with it. The public has learned that I will be there with every ounce of entertainment I can give. I respect my public. You've never seen me, nor heard me, criticize its taste, have you? No one else has. It knows what it wants. It knows what I can give it better than I know myself."

Fred Stone and David Montgomery were a comedy team of unique talent. Will Rogers said of Stone: "He is the only musical comedy comedian that has ever been able to please the children and the grownups, too." The pair is shown in a scene from *The Wizard of Oz*.

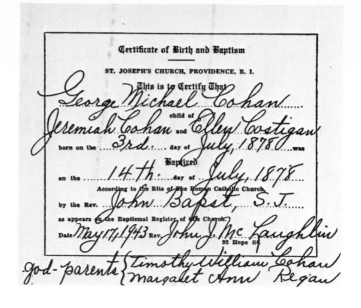

If Harrigan was versatile and appealed to vast numbers of comedy-hungry people, a brash young man who was born and raised in the shadow of the theater was ready to pick up where Harrigan and Hart left off. His name was George M. Cohan, the youngest of the Cohan family of four — a well-known vaudeville act.

Swift-moving and vigorous, Cohan moved into the theatrical world at the turn of the century like a flag-waving tornado. Soon he had the nation singing his tunes and laughing at his jokes. Before he ended his career (although it came late) he was rewarded with the Congressional Medal of Honor by President Roosevelt for writing two of the nation's most popular song hits: *Over There* and *A Grand Old Flag*.

From the start, Cohan refused to become a "mugger" after the fashion of George L. Fox. Instead he substituted his own brand of breeziness and concocted a series of fast-moving plays such as *The Governor's Son, Get-Rich-Quick Wallingford, George Washington, Jr.,* etc. His plays gave the impression of a great machine shooting out characters, choruses, songs, dances with the rapidity of a machine gun.

Known as a song-and-dance man, Cohan almost singlehanded, and out of the corner of his mouth, changed the face of musical comedy and introduced into the theater a flag-waving content which had no equal short of a Fourth of July parade.

Cohan once remarked: "Would you like to know how I write my songs, or rather how I don't write them? I go to bed — while I am sound asleep the spirit moves me — I get up, take pencil and paper in hand. The spirit moves me again and I write and write, line after line. Presto, soon my song is finished."

In a sense, Cohan carries on the traditional Yankee character which had its start in the Jonathan of the earlier days. *Theatre Magazine* stated:

To a large part of the public Cohan represents the restless American spirit, the cheeky go-aheadness of the hustling Yankee. All the time he is on the stage he is in motion. His hat worn jauntily on one side of his head, his face screwed up into a perpetual grin, his legs never still for a moment, coming on with the skit that soon develops into a hilarious dance, singing his own songs with a nasal drawl and forever waving a flag.

50

George M. Cohan, the great song-and-dance man, made frequent use of patriotic themes in his plays. Will Rogers once commented that "Cohan wore out more flags than a war." A plaque at his birthplace in Providence, R. I., set his birthday characteristically at July 4th. A peek at his birth certificate, however, shows the date as July 3rd.

George M. Cohan getting ready for the opening curtain.

Eddie Foy was a genial and capable funnyman. Before he ended his career, he had accumulated a huge following of admirers and enough of his own children (seven) to present an entire family act.

In 1903, Foy became a national hero as a result of his courage in the Iroquois Theater fire in Chicago. Almost six hundred men, women and children lost their lives. Attired in his clown costume, Foy sought to reassure the terrified audience and was among the last to leave the doomed theater alive. Right, an account of the fire and a copy of the theater program which describes the theater as "absolutely fireproof."

Eddie Foy's rise is the story of a bootblack who spent his spare time practicing dancing, singing and acrobatics.

It took me several years to realize that my face wasn't built for tragedy [stated Foy], and that it would be a pity to waste my talents as a dancer and fun-maker. But after I had given up the hope of playing Hamlet and Lear and had made a success in the musical comedy and extravaganza foolery, I still clung to the hope that I might some day do something

Eddie Foy, Comedian, the Real Hero of the Great Fire Tragedy

Actor First Tried to Quiet Audience. Then Saw That Members of His Company Got Out Safely.

(Special to The Commercial Advertiser.)

CHICAGO, Dec. 31.—Every great calamity develops its hero or heroes, and the burning of the Iroquois Theatre has given "Eddie" Foy a name for coolness, presence of mind, clean-cut grit and courage which will be worth much more to him than any fame that has come to him or may come from his fun-making. It is because Foy took command of the situation that the horrible death-roll is not even larger than it is.

With the crackling of the first flames on the stage, out from the wings ran a grotesque figure—fearfully grotesque in the grim surroundings. On his legs were comical tights. About the upper part of his body was a loose, flapping garment, such as actors sometimes wear in the

MISS CHARLOTTE MORTON,
Another of the players in "Blue Beard."

dressing room when making up. His face was painted out of all semblance to its real self and the head was crowned with an absurd wig. Whoever has seen Eddie Foy in "Mr. Bluebeard" knows how he looks with his make-up complete. He is infinitely more comical when it is not finished.

The scene was terrifying. In the wings and up in the flies were the crackling flames. Wisps of smoke swept downward and out into the auditorium. On the stage was a huddled mass of panic-stricken women, pale through the layers of grease paint. In the auditorium, frenzied with fear, was the audience, fighting to get to the door. It was a time when a commander was needed. That commander was the absurd-looking comedian.

"Keep quiet!" he shouted. "Take your seats! There is no danger. Plenty of time to go out quietly!" And then to the leader of the orchestra: "Play! Play!

conclusions of all that had happened. He got over to the Sherman House, where surgeons dressed his badly burned hands, and then, with the reaction, he nearly collapsed.

Foy himself has not yet a very clear idea of all that happened, and a much less clear idea of what he did. Telling

majority of those on the floor got safely out into the open air. Upstairs it was different. Further away from the commanding presence of the comedian and the influence of the playing musicians, conscious that there were stairs to go down, everybody rushed, fighting like savages, to be the first out. That was where death reaped its greatest harvest.

Still cool, seeing that he could do no more to help the audience, he turned his attention to the people on the stage and in the wings. About himself he thought nothing. Before he rushed out on the stage to attempt to stay the panic he had thrown his small son, who was with him, into the arms of a man who carried the boy to the street. The comedian's mind was at rest on that score. No one had thought to lower the asbestos curtain which would confine the fire to the stage. He ordered the "grips" to lower it. Down it began to come—with horrifying slowness—and then it stuck.

That destroyed the last hope of saving the house. The audience, by this time beyond all human control, had to look out for itself. Foy turned his attention to the members of the company, most of whom were standing about dazed with fright. He handled them as a collie dog would handle a flock of sheep. He drove them before him, out of the doors. The fire increased with maniacal energy. It roared through the flimsy stage fittings

little cuts caused by bursting electric lights. I tried to quiet the audience, and told Dillea to keep his men playing. Then I tried to have the asbestos curtain drop, but it stuck. Then I knew there was no hope, and all that could be done was to save as many as possible. The failure of

Iroquois Theatre

ABSOLUTELY FIREPROOF

RANDOLPH Bet. DEARBORN and STATE STS., CHICAGO
IROQUOIS THEATRE CO., PROPRIETORS.
WILL J. DAVIS, and HARRY J. POWERS,
Resident Owners and Managers

Week Beginning Monday, December 7th, 1903

EVERY EVENING INCLUDING SUNDAY
WEDNESDAY AND SATURDAY MATINEES
SPECIAL MATINEE NEW YEARS DAY

KLAW & ERLANGER Present

MR. BLUE BEARD

The Great Spectacular Entertainment from Theatre Royal,
Drury Lane, London.

By J. HICKORY WOOD and ARTHUR COLLINS.
Adapted for the American Stage by JOHN J. McNALLY.
The Lyrics, unless otherwise indicated, by J. Cheever Goodwin.
Music, unless otherwise indicated, by Frederick Solomon.
Ballets by Ernest D'Auban.
Produced under Stage Direction of Herbert Gresham and Ned Wayburn.
Business Direction of Jos. Brooks. Edwin H. Price, Manager.

SYNOPSIS OF SCENES, MUSIC AND INCIDENTS.

ACT I.

Scene 1—The Market Place on the Quay, near Bagdad. (Bruce Smith.)
Mustapha plots to separate Selim and Fatima and sell the beautiful Fatima to the monster Blue Beard. Blue Beard arrives; purchases slaves, Sister Anne falls in love with Blue Beard and spurns Irish Patshaw. Blue Beard seizes Fatima and takes her on board his yacht.

Opening Chorus—
  a. "Come, Buy Our Luscious Fruits."
  b. "Oriental Slaves are we."
  c. "We Come from Dalmatia."
  d. Algerian Slave song and chorus.
  aa. Grand Entrance Blue Beard's Retinue. Medley Ensemble.
  bb. Song—"A most Unpopular Potentate." Blue Beard and Chorus.
  a. "Welcome Fatima."
Song—"I'm As Good as I Ought To Be." Blanche Adams.
Finale—"Then Away We Go."
  Scene 2—On Board Blue Beard's Yacht. (Bruce Smith.)
Fatima with Selim attempts to escape from Blue Beard's yacht but is prevented. Selim jumps overboard
Opening Chorus—"There's Nothing Like the Life we Sailors Lead."
Duet—Miss Rafter and Miss Adams.
Medley—Blue Beard.
"Beautiful World it Would Be." (Harry Von Tilzer.) Harry Gilfoil.

a bit more serious or at least might be permitted to portray the part of that wittiest and most delightful of Shakespeare's jesters, Touchstone. But somehow the managers couldn't see me as a Shakespearian clown.

But Eddie Foy did win himself a very warm spot in the hearts of the American people. Graduating from minstrel shows and beer halls, he turned to vaudeville and musical comedy, where he was a star for thirty years. The critic for the *Dramatic Mirror* said:

Eddie Foy is the mildest, least obtrusive comedian on the stage. His is the art that conceals art. Many comedians draw their laugh-making in the same fashion as a slugger puts his opponent out of breath and vision. They are violently aggressive. . . .

Foy is elusive . . . he defies analysis. It is much easier to say what his art is not than what it is. It does not consist in tumbling nor contortions . . . it does not owe its success to brass lungs nor megaphone delivery.

When you reflect upon what Eddie Foy's art is not, you realize how deep is the art that is to all appearances so narrow. His methods are as gentle as those of a child under the eyes of a watchful mother. If he has ever bellowed on the stage, I have never heard him.

If Foy's humor was gentle, nonaggressive, the same cannot be said for two young men — one tall and one short — who entered the theater when they were nine years old and did not leave it until they had become world-famous and had spanned a period from the beginnings of vaudeville to the coming of radio and motion pictures. They were the famous comedy team of Joe Weber and Lew Fields. From their very start in the early eighties, as Weber himself said, "All the public wanted to see was Fields knock the Hell out of me."

Said Fields, "I don't know why it was but the audience always seemed to have a grudge against him" (meaning Joe Weber). Like so many of their predecessors since the days of Thomas "Daddy" Rice, Weber and Fields started in their careers as blackface comedians. But to win a position in the theater world they showed a maximum flexibility. They composed their lyrics so that they could change them to fit whatever opportunity happened to arise. "Here we are, an Irish pair," they sang, or when another type of comedian was needed, they changed the words to "Here we are, a German pair." From the earliest days the Weber and Fields type of humor was rough and tumble including murdering the English language as well as murdering each other.

Weber and Fields were more than a great comedy combination. They were innovators who pioneered in many new theatrical techniques. Their form of amusement was made up of a combination of hastily improvised comedy, sentimental and witty songs, acrobatics, slapstick, dialect stories, parodies and burlesques.

WEBER AND FIELDS OWN COMPANY

"WHO GETS THE MONEY FIRST, WINS"

When Weber and Fields announced their separation, the news created a furor. The newspapers were full of reports and rumors of the separation and the possibility of a reunion. It wasn't until late in life that the pair rejoined to take part in a network radio show in 1926.

Their humor, while it may be dated now, was hilarious then:

"Who is that lady I saw you with last night?" asked Weber.

"She ain't no lady, she's my wife," answered Fields while the audience roared. The echoes of that one still persist in the land.

During a presidential election year Fields declared that he had known all along that Harrison would defeat Cleveland. Weber challenged the statement. Lew pointed to the number of Harrison banners he had seen.

"Banners don't vote!" Joe retorted.

"They show which way the wind blows," was Lew's snapper.

A typical Weber and Fields exchange went like this.

Mike: I am delightfulness to meet you.
Myer: Der disgust is all mine.
Mike: I receivedidid a letter from mein goil, but I don't know how to writteninin her back.
Myer: Writteninin her back! Such an edumuncation you got it? Writteninin her back! You mean rotteninin her back. How can you answer her ven you don't know how to write?

56

WEBER AND FIELDS

"TALK IT ALL OVER" AND TELL THE REAL STORY OF THEIR FRIENDSHIP AND ESTRANGEMENT THEIR HITS AND MISSES AND WHAT BROUGHT ABOUT
THEIR SEPARATION

QUARRELS REND THE WEBERFIELDS

Mann and Fields Do Not Speak and Fields and Weber Are Sharply at Odds.

TOUR MAY CLOSE ABRUPTLY

...ber &
...st ad-
...have
...y are
...ult in
...tour.
...fields
...oseph
"It's
...okes
...hom

WEBER AND FIELDS TO BE REUNITED?

Theatrical Circles Hear That Differences Between the Comedians May Be Bridged

MR. WEBER'

Asks Mr. Fields
Him at $

A very pleasan...
circles yesterday...
ners of the days...
Hall will come...
Petted by the...
tained in rare g...
finally being co...
managers of N...
individual for...
they were par...
of their own...
them gradual...
further ra...
It w...
publi...
has
had

WEBER & FIELDS WILL NOT PART

Managers Deny All Rumors to This Effect and Say They Will Continue as Heretofore.

BOTH PARTNERS ARE IN ACCORD

Stories to the effect that Weber & Fields are to sever their partnership, appear to have been unwarranted, in view of the following dispatch received last night by The Morning Telegraph:

Omaha, Neb, March 4.
Morning Telegraph, N. Y.:

We desire to make this statement regarding the published reports in various New York papers to the effect that there has been a quarrel, a contemplated sale of the music hall and removal of the entertainment to the Casino. We wish to state positively, without reservation of any sort, that these rumors are absolutely without foundation, and the partnership which has existed for twenty ... years will be continued. ... this denial the promin-...as been accorded the ...that have surely ema-...some interested person. ...EBER and LEW M...

WEBER AND FIELDS ARE PARTNERS AGAIN

Comedians, After Seven Y... Separation, Agree to R... ganize Their Old Compa...

New Partnership Only for th... pany They Will Appear In-... Has Separate Ente...

Weber and Fie...
...nce a...

WEBER SAVED FIELDS' LIFE

It's an Old Story, but Serves to Adorn a Fresh Denial.

(Special Dispatch to The Morning Telegraph.)

CHICAGO, March 28.—Lew Fields for the steenth time denied that he would separate from Joe Weber, before leaving for Pittsburg this afternoon.

"No, we are not going to separate," said Fields. "I am going to cling to the little fellow as he clung to me twenty-seven years ago. We had just closed i... Memphis and left the town witho... cent between us. We hit the ti... some twel... miles out of M... struck... train a... I sa...

Mike: Dot makes no nefer mind. She don't know how to read.

Myer: If you luf her, vy don't you send her some poultry?

Mike: She don't need no poultry; her father is a butcher.

Myer: I mean luf voids like Romeo und Chuliet talks.

        If you luf you like I luf me

        No knife can cut us togedder.

Mike: I don't like dot.

Myer: Vell, vot do you vant to say to her?

Mike: I don't vant you to know vat I'm saying to her. All I vant you to do is to tell me vot to put in her letter.

Myer: Such a foolishness you are! If I don't tell you vot to say, how vill you know vot to write if she don't know how to read?

Mike: I don't vant nobody to know vot I'm writteninin to her.

Myer: You don't vant anyone to know vot you are rotteninin?

Mike: No.

Myer: Then send her a postal card.

Mike: Send her a postal card? If I do she'll think I don't care two cendts for her.

Myer: Are you going to marry her?

Mike: In two days I vill be a murdered man.

Myer: Vot?

Mike: I mean a married man.

Myer: I hope you vill always look back upon der presendt moment as der habbiest moment uff your life.

Mike: But I aind't married yet.

Myer: I know it, und furdermore, upon dis suspicious occasion, I also vish to express to you — charges collect — my uppermost depreciation of der dishonor you haf informed upon me in making me your bridesmaid.

Mike: Der insuldt is all mein.

Although Weber and Fields may appear today to be merely another slapstick team, actually they were innovators of the most influential kind. Until they came upon the scene, the usual comedy was either pure slapstick, or mere gag patter. Weber and Fields were among the first to base their comedy on actual realism, combining slapstick with sharp social satire. The theater was not the same after they were finished with it.

They were innovators in many other ways. Continuing the trend started by Mrs. Keith, they would have nothing to do with vulgarity. Their shows were clean and they were proud to boast of this. Weber and Fields were among the first to introduce the notion of women being permitted to attend theatrical productions. When they were playing in Colonel Jim Fennessey's Peoples Theatre in Cincinnati, the attendance was, as usual, strictly stag. The bar to the presence of women was not what happened on the stage but the drinking, smoking male audience. As a result, the men would return home carrying reports about the good things of vaudeville or the stage and the women would have nothing but complaints that the men should monopolize this form of entertainment.

Fields suggested to Colonel Fennessey that one night a week be set aside when smoking and drinking be banned and women admitted. Fennessey was aghast. "Let sleeping dogs lie, son," he said pleadingly, "Let 'em in here once and they'll be pushing in regular the first thing you know and driving the boys away. A man likes to have some place where he can get away from petticoats."

But Fields insisted and finally the Colonel reluctantly agreed that "we might re-serve the boxes for them some night and let a few in through the stage door." But Weber and Fields were not satisfied. "Why not do the thing up brown and get it talked about?" they asked. "Get out a lot of dodgers announcing Friday as 'Ladies' Night'; no smoking, no drinking and a cut flower presented to every lady present. Give the old house a thorough scrubbing and fill your lobby with flowers. Try it once." Fennessey grunted, "It's a crazy idea and against my better judgment, but have your own way."

Friday came and ten charwomen attacked the old theater with brushes and soap. By night the theater was gleamingly clean. The ladies were admitted and from that time on, the theater was never again to recapture its former bachelor freedom. "Ladies' Night" became a Cincinnati institution and Weber and Fields had done it.

So well associated were the names of Weber and Fields that America looked upon them interchangeably. As Weber himself recalled:

> If I use the telephone, the conversation will run something like this:
> "This is Joe Weber speaking."
> "Who?"
> "Weber — Joe Weber."
> "I don't get the name."
> "Joe Weber of Weber and Fields."
> "Oh yes, Mr. Weber."

Lew and I have answered to either Weber or to Fields for forty years. "Glad to meet you, Mr. Weber," a man says on shaking my hand; "Goodbye, Mr. Fields" when he leaves. My wife and I are used to being introduced as Mr. Weber and Mrs. Fields. Lew and I sometimes wonder if they will get our names straight on our tombstones.

59

Coincidentally, like McIntyre and Heath, Weber and Fields died within a year of each other. Lew Fields passed away in 1941, and the year following, his partner of so many years, Joe Weber, joined him.

All was not clear sailing, however. Weber and Fields' partnership was tragically dissolved one night with the final performance of the show *Whoop-dee-doo*. Midst the weeping of chorus girls and major publicity, the announcement was made that the famed team was going to break up. Wrote the *Herald*:

A demonstration unique in theatrical history marked the ringing down of the last curtain. An audience which filled the large new theatre and composed of representatives of society clubdom, the world of first night, the theatre in every walk of life called for the curtain to rise again. Then in response to demands, speeches were made by members of the stock company in which the two men who had made Weber and Fields a household word were told that they were committing business suicide; were told that they were making a grievous mistake, amid cries of "Right, right."
A Broadway audience is not particularly sentimental, but the tears that streaked the painted and powdered faces of the stage were multiplied many times in the audience as "Auld Lang Syne" became the final musical number.

The split between Weber and Fields became the subject of national discussion, heralded in all the papers, a national catastrophe.

Few teams of comedians in the history of the theater achieved the place in the hearts of so many people as the team of Weber and Fields in their prime. The theater was somehow not the same after the pair separated.

Significantly, Lew Fields kept the Weber and Fields Theater open for several years after the split, taking into temporary partnership a young man from Chicago who seemed to have an eye for showmanship and women — especially women.

His name was Florenz Ziegfeld.

60

6

From Follies to Flickers

Theatre

42nd Street, West of Broadway

The New Amsterdam Theatre Planned and Designed by A. L. Erlanger, Architects. and F. Richard Anderson, and Executed by Herts and Tallant, Architects. ERLANGER, DILLINGHAM & ZIEGFELD Lessees and Managers

NOTICE: This Theatre, with every seat occupied, can be emptied in less than three minutes. Choose NOW the Exit nearest to your seat, and in case of fire walk (do not run) to that Exit.
THOMAS J. DRENNAN, Fire Commissioner.

WEEK BEGINNING MONDAY EVENING, SEPTEMBER 11, 1922
Matinees Wednesday and Saturday

FLORENZ ZIEGFELD, JR.
Offers the Sixteenth of the Series of
THE NATIONAL INSTITUTION GLORIFYING THE AMERICAN GIRL

ZIEGFELD FOLLIES

STAGED BY NED WAYBURN

Music by Victor Herbert, Louis A. Hirsch and Dave Stamper
Lyrics by Gene Buck Book by Ring Lardner and Ralph Spence
"Sicilian" and "Frolicking Gods" Ballets arranged by Fokine
Scenes by Joseph Urban and Others.
Produced Under the Supervision of Ziegfeld, Jr.
Orchestra Under Direction of

VISITORS TO
Who Missed
MAY SE
The Ziegfeld
MARILYN MILLER an

"SAL
Now P
AT THE C
(Opposite Histor

SCENE 1—"BLUNDERLAND" (Pr
(By Ralph Spence; Lyrics by

1st WEEK—BEGINNING WEDNESDAY EVENING, FEB. 9.

FLORENZ ZIEGFELD, JR.
OFFERS FOR YOUR ENTERTAINMENT THE

ZIEGFELD MIDNIGHT FROLIC

(11th of the Series)
STAGED BY EDWARD ROYCE
WRITTEN BY BALLARD MACDONALD
COMPOSED BY HARRY CARROLL
SCENES BY JOSEPH URBAN
Conceived and produced under the personal supervision of
F. Ziegfeld, Jr.
Orchestra under the direction of Max Hoffman
PART I.

1 OPENING—
"The Compère"

HERBERT HO
KATHLENE MART
Sung by HERBERT HO
Perle Germonde
Pearl Eaton
Gladys Loftus
Olive Osborne
Lillian Mackenzie
Beatrice Milner
Blanche Parks
Avonne Taylor
Alma Mamay
Albertine Marlowe
Mildred Sinclair
Martha Pierre
Sung by ANNETTE BADE
Margaret Falconer, Helen
lfs, Beatrice Savage, Betty
Haver, Louise Stafford and

an Hupfeld ANNA WHEATON

EXT PAGE FOLLOWING

WEEK BEGINNING MONDAY EVENING, MARCH 8, 1920

FLORENZ ZIEGFELD, JR.
PRESENTS THE SECOND

ZIEGFELD NINE O'CLOCK REVUE

ENTITLED

ZIEGFELD GIRLS OF 1920

STAGED BY NED WAYBURN

LYRICS BY GENE BUCK and MUSIC BY DAVE STAMPER
DECORATIONS AND SCENIC INVESTITURE BY JOSEPH URBAN

Conceived and Produced under the Personal Supervision of
feld, Jr.

GRAM
SERVED WHILE THE
IS BEING GIVEN
I.
OF YESTERDAY,"
MR. JOHN PRICE JONES
E MERRY MERRY,"

New Amsterdam Theatre

42nd Street, West of Broadway

The New Amsterdam Theatre Planned and Designed by A. L. Erlanger and F. Richard Anderson, and Executed by Herts and Tallant, Architects.
NEWAM THEATRE CORPORATION
ERLANGER, DILLINGHAM & ZIEGFELD,
Directors

NOTICE: This Theatre, with every seat occupied, can be emptied in less than three minutes. Choose NOW the Exit nearest to your seat, and in case of fire walk (do not run) to that Exit.
THOMAS J. DRENNAN, Fire Commissioner.

WEEK BEGINNING MONDAY EVENING, SEPTEMBER 8, 1924
Matinees Wednesday and Saturday

The temperature of this theatre is made thoroughly comfortable in the hottest weather by the forcing of purified air through tons of ice by gigantic high-pressure revolving fans.

FLORENZ ZIEGFELD
Presents the 19th Annual Production Made in America of
The National Institution

ZIEGFELD FOLLIES
GLORIFYING THE AMERICAN GIRL

Staged by JULIAN MITCHELL

Dialogue by
William Anthony McGuire and Will Rogers
Lyrics by
Gene Buck and Joseph J. McCarthy
Music by
Victor Herbert, Raymond Hubbell, Dave Stamper, Harry Tier
and Dr. Albert Szirmai
Tableaux Devised and Staged by
Ben Ali Haggin
Orchestra Under Direction of
Victor Baravalle
Produced by F. ZIEGFELD

At the SELWYN Theatre
EDDIE CANTOR in "KID BOOTS" with MARY EAT
Ziegfeld's Greatest Musical Comedy
Popular Priced Matinees—Thursday and Satur

ACT 1.
THE BEAUTY FLOAT
by BEN ALI HAGGIN
Knapp, and the Goodwin

NEW AMSTERDAM THEATRE

MARINE ROOF
HOTEL BOSSERT, Montague-Hicks-Remsen Sts., Broc

Delightful Dining in the Open Air—
Most Unique Roof and View in America.

Dancing every evening, except Sunday, 6 P. M. to clos
Every Sunday evening, Special Musical Program 6 to 10 P

Complete Protection from the Weather

Motor over the Manhattan Bridge, take first turn to the right an
south on Hicks Street; or Subway to Borough Hall.

Burton F. White, Proprietor
F. D. Ray, Jr., Associate

PROGRAM CONTINUED

ACT II.
Scene 13—"The Lower Regions."
Characters.
His Satanic Majesty (added lines written by himself) WILL ROGER
Head Clerk FRANK CARTE
The Girl in Hell ALLYN KIN
Bell Boy
A Profiteer KATHRYN PERRY
New York Society Woman HARRY KELL
A Dancing Girl "DOLORES
Eve ANN PENNINGTON
Twin Imps KAY LAUREL
Liberty Loan Slacker FAIRBANKS TWINS
Somebody's Sweetheart CLAY HILL
Senator La Follette W. C. FIELDS
IMPS—Wood, Poole, Harrison, Braham, Bell, Shelly, DOROTHY LEEDS
SHE DEVILS—Virginia, Robinson, Morton, Brady, Leisy, Richardson,
Ullman, Lloyd.
Demons, Male Dancers.
Inventor of Comedy Bicycles BILLIE RITCHIE
Assisted by Male Principals
Scene 14.
Song—"Mine Was a Marriage of Convenience" MARILYN MILLER
"Billie Burke"

PROGRAM CONTINUED ON SECOND PAGE FOLLOW

When Weber and Fields split, the dapper young man with a flair for showmanship who stepped into the breach was to glorify more chorus girls and comedians than any producer up to his time . . . or since.

Scarcely had show business entered the twentieth century when it encountered Ziegfeld, who proceeded to build a new form of American theatrical presentation which he labeled the *Ziegfeld Follies*.

In the name of glorifying the American girl, Ziegfeld stripped her of her clothes and had her walk around the stage with a huge fan and a haughty look. Ziegfeld's formula for his new type of revue was simple: first, beautiful girls; second, good comedians; and third, lush backgrounds.

His *Follies* were eye-filling spectacles which raided musical comedy and vaudeville for beautiful women and funny laugh makers. The first *Ziegfeld Follies* opened in 1907. One year later, Tony Pastor, the man who had done more to found present-day vaudeville than any other single person, died leaving very little personal fortune.

The fact that the *Ziegfeld Follies* was the source of some of the greatest comic genius in the history of the American theater was more accidental than planned. Ziegfeld was no judge of comedy nor did he profess to be. His main talent was judging womanflesh.

He rarely smiled at his comedians although in the years that the *Ziegfeld Follies* held sway, from 1907 to 1931, he featured such fun makers as Leon Errol, Bert Williams, Fanny Brice, George Bickell, Frank Tinney, Ed Wynn, W. C. Fields, Nat Wills, Eddie Cantor, Will Rogers, Ed Gallagher and Al Shean, Ray Dooley, Bert Wheeler, Willie Howard, etc.

Ziegfeld was, however, much more interested in hips than quips and the fact that he did help celebrate many a comedian was merely a by-product of his American-girl glorification factory.

Ziegfeld owed much to American burlesque. As George Jean Nathan said at the time:

The loudest and most popular laughter in the American theatres of today is provoked by humor that has been graduated from burlesque . . . the leading comedians of a dozen or more shows of uniformly high prosperity throughout the country have come to the more urgent stage from burlesque, and have brought their wheezes with them.

Among the most popular comedians whom the *Ziegfeld Follies* brought forward was Bert Williams. He had a unique way of rendering songs: injecting his talk between rests and catching up with the melodic phrase after he had let it get a head start.

Williams was the first Negro entertainer since the early nineties to appear in an all-white show before southern audiences. He was a natural-born mimic as well as a singer and dancer. Despite the fact that he was dark-skinned, he used the traditional burnt cork make-up when on stage.

Discussing his comedy role, Williams told a friend, "Speaking of new laughs, they are only younger than the old ones, and not quite so sincere. Did you ever hear of the origin of Joe Miller's joke book? You know, it was found in the library of Noah's Ark."

Before entering the *Follies* Williams achieved national prominence as a comedian and dancer in combination with George Walker. His fame even spread abroad, and when he was at the Shaftsebury Theatre in London, Williams was invited to attend a lawn party at Buckingham Palace to entertain the guests at a birthday party of King Edward VII. It was on this occasion that Williams was able to teach the king the elements of the American Cake Walk.

According to Eddie Cantor, "Bert Williams was one of the finest artists. . . . His knack for rhythmic timing . . . has never been excelled."

Williams was the hit of the *Follies* during the early years. "I'm just out here to give the gals time to change," he would tell the audience.

One of the greatest comic acts of all times was the combination of Bert Williams and Leon Errol, a great comedian in his own right. In the *Follies* of 1911, the pair took part in a skit, "Upper and Lower Level." The scene was in New York's Grand Central Station and Williams would play the part of a redcap while Errol was a Major Waterbrush.

The act started with precisely four written lines and then Williams and Errol would carry on, ad libbing, improvising, creating such hilarity through their pantomiming and spontaneous humor as to stretch an act which was to last but a few minutes to almost half an hour.

According to the report, the manager wired Ziegfeld, who was in Chicago at the time, that the pair threatened to disorganize the entire show. Ziegfeld wired back curtly to curb them. But the situation was beyond the control of the manager.

When Ziegfeld returned East, he had every intention of knocking the troublesome act from the *Follies* repertoire. But as he stood in the rear of the theater personally watching the pair, he was unable to restrain his own laughter, although he was not usually one to enjoy the jokes of his own comedians. The act of Williams and Errol stayed.

During his lifetime, Williams was called "The Son of Laughter" and "King of Comedy."

"He was one of the kindest, most amenable and most likable men that I have ever known," said David Belasco, famous theatrical producer, "and I have known many. He was a delightful entertainer. He was a sincere and careful ,artist and a genuine comedian."

According to Ring Lardner: "If you had seen him just dance in the old days, you'd have pronounced him 'comedian and clown' as well as champion eccentric hoofer of all time. In my regard he leads the league as a comedian and can be given no worse than a tie for first place for a clown, pantomimist, story-teller, eccentric dancer and singer of a certain type of song."

W. C. Fields, himself a comic star of the *Follies,* thought Williams "the funniest man I ever saw and the saddest man I ever saw. I often wonder whether other people sensed what I did in him — the deep undercurrent of pathos."

Eddie Cantor, who made a name for himself as a comedian in the *Follies* too, says:

Bert Williams was not only a great comic, but extremely human and possessed of fine sensibilities. It happened in St. Louis that he walked up to a bar and asked for gin.

The bartender, reluctant to serve a Negro, said, "I'll give you gin, but it's fifty dollars a glass."

Bert Williams quietly took out his billfold and produced a $500 bill.

"Give me ten of them," he said.

Booker T. Washington, famous Negro educator, once said: "Bert Williams has done more for the race than I have. He has smiled his way into people's hearts. I have been obliged to *fight* my way."

Another of Ziegfeld's great comic characters was Fanny Brice, who fought her way upward from amateur-night contests to become one of the great comediennes in American theatrical history.

Fanny was one of the few girls hired by Ziegfeld for reasons other than their beauty. What Fanny lacked by Ziegfeld's standards, however, she made up in her quick mind, expressive eyes and comic spirit. Fanny had a sense of caricature which was nothing short of brilliant. She could lampoon anyone from a fan dancer to an evangelist. Fanny Brice was in almost every *Follies* from 1910 to 1923. When the *Ziegfeld Midnight Frolic* started on the Amsterdam Roof, Fanny was in that. She would play the regular *Follies,* then go upstairs with other selected members of the cast to do the *Frolic.*

There was a radio program many years ago called *Ziegfeld Follies on the Air.* Fanny was a star in that. When they made the movie *The Great Ziegfeld* in Hollywood, Fanny was in it. When *The Ziegfeld Follies* was made as a picture, Fanny participated. And when the Shuberts revived the *Follies,* shortly after Ziegfeld died, Fanny headed the cast.

Fanny had an assortment of grotesque expressions which she used interchangeably. Some thought Fanny's success was due to the way she contrasted with the beauties whom Ziegfeld carefully collected for his chorus. But it could not have been that because Fanny was funny when she was appearing by herself whether on the radio as her seven-year-old "Baby Snooks," in the motion picture, in a musical revue or a *Ziegfeld Follies.*

Although Fanny was a singer, Ziegfeld was soon to find out that she was much more. Her talent for burlesque and satire made her the outstanding satirist of the

Florenz Ziegfeld "glorified" the American chorus girl. He also helped develop many top comedians. Harry Watson, Jr., was a funnyman of the 1907 *Follies.*

66

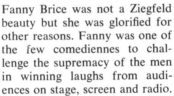

Fanny Brice was not a Ziegfeld beauty but she was glorified for other reasons. Fanny was one of the few comediennes to challenge the supremacy of the men in winning laughs from audiences on stage, screen and radio.

American theater during her era. Certainly among women comedians she was supreme. Her lampoon of Theda Bara, the vamp of silent movie days, or her take-off of Camille, accompanied by W. C. Fields, or her hilarious comic interpretations of the "Dying Swan" ballet — these were memorable performances. No wonder Fanny Brice became the star of the *Ziegfeld Follies* which specialized in presenting stars of many kinds.

On the subject of comedy, Fanny would say:

You get your first laugh — boom! you're going. You lose yourself, you become whatever it is they're laughing at, but it isn't you. Anytime I ever did any kind of dance, don't you think that in my heart, as I am making them laugh, that I don't want them to say: "She's really so graceful"?

If you're a comic you have to be nice. And the audience has to like you. You have to have a softness about you, because if you do comedy and you are harsh, there is something offensive about it. Also you must set up your audience for the laugh you are working for. So you go along and everything is fine, like any other act, and then — boom! you give it to them. Like there is a beautiful painting of a woman and you paint a mustache on her.

One of the funniest scenes people remember from the *Follies* featured the comedian, Leon Errol, who made a specialty of imitating a typical drunk whether it was a sailor, a husband, a cowboy or even Louis XIV.

Now, Errol's claim to comedian fame was not based on the cleverness of his lines or his songs or his gag delivery. As he himself said, he didn't care very much whether he had lines to speak or not. Errol's chief stock in trade was his own personalized type of stagger dancing which defied the laws of equilibrium. By a strange kind of buckling of his rubbery legs, he led to the belief that he would not be able to stand a moment longer, continuing his careening from one end of the stage to the other.

In one particular skit the "intoxicated" Errol found himself in a dancing school as Ziegfeld's beautiful glorified girls entered for a tango lesson. Errol assumed them to be customers in a Turkish bath, and they took him to be a dancing teacher.

Rising to the occasion, his eyes glazing as he glanced over the bevy of half-dressed beauties, he led the chorus in an hilarious scene of buffoonery.

"Do what I do," he shouted to the chorus as he swayed about, rolling on the floor, staggering to his feet only to collapse again.

In discussing this famous scene Errol said:

A great deal of the fun of that scene was in the strained, anxious faces of the pupils. They knew they had to do everything I did, stagger when I staggered, roll on the floor when I rolled, sit down when I sat down and flop when I flopped.

I had rehearsed each girl separately for hours. They were letter perfect, foot perfect. But after they had thoroughly learned the dance and I had numbered the changes in the steps, I warned them that I wouldn't follow that order. Every night I would vary the dance. Number 9 might come in on Thursday night where Number 7 had been on Tuesday. That is the reason they were so painfully intent on every step I took.

Bobby Clark was another *Follies* comedian. The combination of Clark and Paul McCullough (left) was one of the more successful comedy partnerships.

Leon Errol, the little man with the rubber legs, was a Ziegfeld laugh maker for many years.

While Ziegfeld was not an enthusiast for comedians, there was one whom he appreciated.

When in town, Ziegfeld rarely missed an opportunity to watch Will Rogers work. "You know," Ziegfeld once said, "I'm not supposed to have a very quick sense of humor. Half the great comedians that I've had in my shows, that I paid a lot of money to who made my customers shriek, were not only not funny to me, but I couldn't understand why they seemed funny to anybody. But this Rogers, I never miss him if I can help it, though you'd be surprised at how many of my expensive comics I've run out on and locked myself in my office when they were on the stage."

Rogers had his start as a trick roper and not as a comedian. As a matter of fact, Rogers had as his ambition to become the world's greatest roper and he nearly achieved his ambition. The fact that he developed into a comedian was more or less accidental.

The humor of Will Rogers dates back to the early Jonathan type. Rogers is the natural continuation of the rough-and-ready Yankee, reveling in his crude wisdom, homely humor and contempt for pomp and hypocrisy.

When Rogers first broke in with the *Follies* he was so nervous that a fellow actor advised him to chew gum. This Rogers did, although he never chewed when off the stage. He would simply park his gum on a convenient dressing table or other secret spot and pick it up just before he went on stage.

Rogers seldom rehearsed with the *Follies*. He would follow a policy of studying the current news, going over it carefully prior to his performance. It was for this reason that his performances were of as great interest to his fellow entertainers as to the audience itself.

One of Rogers' earliest jokes from the stage took place when he was twirling a rope in vaudeville. During a lull, he remarked carelessly to the audience: "Swingin' a rope's all right — if your neck ain't in it."

The audience was taken by surprise by his casual comment and roared with laughter. Following the performance, Rogers was abashed and vowed never to speak again, but to carry on his roping act completely in silence. However, his fellow entertainers convinced him that he should employ, as part of his roping act, some of the jokes and humorous anecdotes that he was forever using when off the stage. It was this combination of roping and joking that won him an appearance before Ziegfeld.

In those early days Rogers was far from confident that he would have sufficient gags to keep his audience laughing. He went so far as to keep in his back pocket a little memorandum, which he entitled "Gags for Missing the Horse's Nose," in which he had listed eight little reminders of funny things to say. He found, however, that by studying the newspapers he was able to find enough humorous situations to keep him well supplied with ammunition. Soon he had mastered the technique of maintaining a sufficient reservoir of humorous sayings to keep him in good supply during his entire routine.

When the *New York Times* disavowed responsibility for one of Will Rogers' daily columns, he solemnly disavowed responsibility for the newspaper's entire editorial policy.

Mr. Rogers Is Tolerant and Aloof As Regards Editorial Writers

To the Editor of The New York Times:

BEVERLY HILLS, Cal., Dec. 7.— I would like to state to the readers of THE NEW YORK TIMES that I am in no way responsible for the editorial or political policy of this paper.

I allow them free reign as to their opinion, so long as it is within the bounds of good subscription gathering.

But I want it distinctly understood that their policy may be in direct contrast to mine.

Their editorials may be put in purely for humor, or just to fill space.

Every paper must have its various entertaining features, and their editorials are not always to be taken seriously, and never to be construed as my policy.

Yours,

WILL ROGERS.

Will Rogers was frequently quoted on the floor of Congress. However, on one occasion he was sharply criticized.

When a gentleman quoted me on the floor of Congress the other day [he reported], another member took exception and said he objected to the remarks of a Professional Joke Maker going into the Congressional Record.

Now can you beat that for jealousy among people in the same line? Calling me a Professional Joke Maker! He is right about everything but the Professional. *They* are the Professional Joke Makers. Read some of the Bills that they have passed, if you think they warn't Joke Makers. I could study all my life and not think up half the amount of funny things they can think of in one Session of Congress. Besides, my jokes don't do anybody any harm. You don't have to pay any attention to them. But every one of the jokes these Birds make is a *Law* and hurts somebody (generally everybody).

"Joke Maker"! He couldn't have coined a better term for Congress if he had been inspired. But I object to being called a Professional. I am an Amateur beside them. If I had that Guy's unconscious Humor, Ziegfeld couldn't afford to pay me I would be so funny.

Rogers made his major emphasis on politics and he was able to present his observations in quick and sure and homely phrases. A growing number of people looked upon Rogers as sort of an ideal American statesman and he was seriously suggested for every office including that of President.

"There's already too many comedians in Washington," he replied laughing. "Competition would be too keen for me."

Nothing seemed to faze Rogers. His good humor and natural simplicity seemed to remove the barb of sharpness from his jokes. On one occasion he was the main speaker at a convention of bankers. He started off his remarks by saying: "You're as fine a group of men as ever foreclosed on a widow. I am glad to be with you Shylocks."

Will Rogers shown in an unusual picture roping a goat. Whether roping or acting, Rogers was always natural and unaffected. Pictures on opposite page are from a 1920 film *Jes' Call Me John* with Irene Rich; and *A Connecticut Yankee in King Arthur's Court.*

Most people think of me as a gagman [Rogers once declared]. You have to be funny to keep them listening and reading. I'm just an ignerant feller without any education, so to speak, but I try to know what I'm talking about. I joke to the public, but I do a lot of studying because, though I hand out a lot of foolishness, I don't want to hand out stuff that might be misleading.

I read editorials a lot and while I'm reading them the thought comes to me that I can get this bit of news into the minds of the audience only in a different way. When I go to a national convention, I have to know what they're talking about to know what's funny.

If I were just a clown, Borah and Reed and Mellon and all those fellows wouldn't take the trouble to explain what they're driving at to me. I never worked harder in my life than at the London Disarmament Conference.

I ain't for anything. I look at all of them and I laugh at all of them but I don't advocate. I haven't hardly any politics. Of course, I do belong to the Democratic Party, but even the best of us has got to let a little cussedness come out now and then.

It's a terribly hard job. The guys that tell you they can be funny at any minute, without any effort, are guys that ain't funny to anybody but themselves. I depend on the newspapers for most of my inspirations. Some days there is material for several good lines. Then there may be a week when there isn't a little thing worth mentioning. About once a month I turn out a gag that I get a big kick out of myself. That's a pretty good average.

Once, Oklahoma University was considering Will Rogers for an honorary degree of Doctor of Letters. Rogers heard of the proposition and commented:

There is only one statue of a comedian in Statuary Hall in the nation's Capitol. It is of Will Rogers. Others of the seventy-five statues include Sam Adams, John Calhoun, George Washington, Daniel Webster, and Roger Williams. The statue of Rogers is the only one showing pants in need of pressing.

Will Rogers was F.D.R.'s favorite comedian, invited to the White House five times between 1933 and 1935. No other humorist was in the White House as often during this period. Picture shows President Franklin D. Roosevelt, William G. Mc-Adoo and Rogers.

WILL ROGERS

74

"What are you trying to do, make a joke out of college degrees? They are in bad enough repute as it is, without handing them around to comedians. The whole honorary degree thing is hooey. My limit is a plain A.D., Doctor of Applesauce."

Rogers, of course, considered politicians fair game for his wit. And they, from President to the Senate and the Congress, had to take it. For example, when a certain wealthy gentleman declared that he was running for Congress, Rogers quipped: "He is the only person we can send to Congress who can go into a Fifth Avenue home without delivering something."

Once the idea hit Rogers that nothing useful was being done with the chewing gum consumed in this country. The thought came to him when he visited the home of Mr. Wrigley, the chewing gum magnate, and he was struck with the realization that to succeed nowadays everybody must have an "idea." As Rogers put it:

I just thought to myself, if Bill Wrigley can amass this colossal fortune and pay the manufacturing charges, why can't I do something with secondhand gum? I will have no expense, only the accumulation of the gum after it is thoroughly masticated. Who would be the most beneficial to mankind, the man who invented chewing gum, or me who can find a use for it? Why, say, if I can take a wad of old gum and graft it onto some other substance, I will be the modern Burbank. (With the ideas I have got for used gum I may be honored by my native State of Oklahoma by being made Governor with the impeachment clause scratched out of the Contract.)
All Wrigley had was an Idea. He was the first man to discover that the American Jaws must wag. So why not give them something to wag against? That is, put in a kind of Shock Absorber.
If it wasn't for chewing gum, Americans would wear their teeth off just hitting them against each other. Every Scientist has been figuring out who the different races descend from. I don't know about the other Tribes, but I do know that the American Race descended from the Cow. And Wrigley was smart enough to furnish the Cud. He has made the whole World chew for Democracy. . . .

Will Rogers was one of the most versatile of all American comedians. Not only was he an outstanding star on vaudeville and in the *Follies* but he doubled for Fred Stone, his close friend, in a musical revue when Stone broke his legs in an accident. Rogers altogether made some twenty-four silent films and a number of motion pictures of the talkie variety. Discussing his advent into the movies, Rogers commented, "Well, there was a move on foot for making fewer and worse pictures so they hired me."

Writing from Hollywood on how he broke into the movies, Rogers said:

Out here in Hollywood they say you're not a success unless you owe $50,000 to somebody, have five cars, can develop temperament without notice or reason at all, and been mixed up in four divorce cases and two breach of promise cases.
Well, as a success in Hollywood, I'm a rank failure and I guess I'm too old to teach new tricks and besides I'm pretty well off domestically speaking and ain't yearnin' for a change.

And it was true. As his close friend Marie Dressler, a comedian in her own right, said, "He is practically the only public figure I know who has kept his hair, his wife, and his sense of humor twenty-five years."

One of Will Rogers' comedian teammates in several of the *Ziegfeld Follies* was the former juggler and unique comedian, W. C. Fields.

Outside of being on the same payroll, Will Rogers and Fields had very little in common although both were comedians of major stature.

William Claud Dukinfield, as W. C. Fields was named at birth, was one of a number of jugglers turned comedian, a list which includes Fred Allen, Eddie Cantor and Jimmy Savo.

In his excellent book Robert Lewis Taylor characterizes Fields as "the greatest comic artist ever known." Fields described himself as "the greatest juggler on earth." He set out to be the world's best juggler as Will Rogers had been equally determined to be the world's best roper. And like Rogers he became one of the world's funniest comedians.

Ziegfeld took Fields out of vaudeville for the 1915 edition of the *Follies*. Although he served his term from 1915 to 1921, W. C. Fields never obtained top booking as a comedian, always giving way to Fanny Brice, Will Rogers, Eddie Cantor or Bert Williams.

Unlike Will Rogers, who carried over in his own way the homespun Yankee humor of an earlier Jonathan, Fields apparently started something of a new school of humor. It brought about many imitators but none could match his urbane rascality and hen-pecked aloofness from the world of ordinary mortals. His closest comic ancestor is probably Mark Twain's Colonel Sellers.

W. C. Fields began his career as a juggler, and a good one. Fields achieved international prominence and was often billed "The Greatest Comedian in the World" even though he never said a word throughout his act. Ed Wynn is given the credit for encouraging Fields to accompany his juggling with jokes.

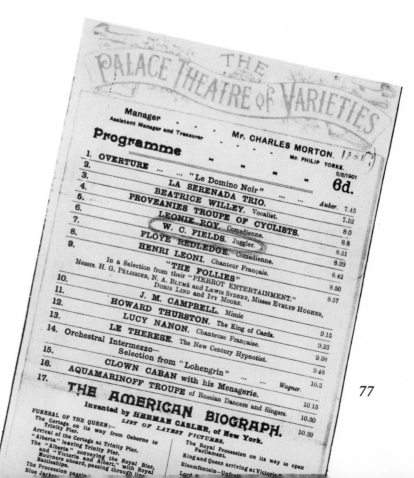

Fields played the part of a ring-master in the picture *Tillie's Punctured Romance*. The lady is Babe London.

Ziegfeld never was able to appreciate Fields' brand of humor and considered him something of a fill-in, to occupy space and time while the girls were changing what little clothes they wore from scene to scene. On one occasion at the close of one of Fields' sketches, Ziegfeld inquired how long it took. He was informed that it took approximately one half hour.

"How long does it take the girls to dress for the next scene?" Ziegfeld asked.

"Seven minutes," was the answer.

"Cut the sketch to seven minutes," ordered Ziegfeld.

Fields never fully recovered from this unkind appraisal. Shortly afterward he moved his field of activities to Hollywood where he won a national following as one of the nation's outstanding comedians.

Sometimes Fields would do more than act in plays and would actually write them under an odd assortment of pen names such at Otis Criblecoblis or Mahatma Kane Jeeves or simply Charles Vogle.

The Fields brand of humor defies careful analysis. The way he walked, the way he carried his cane, his tendency to juggle odd objects, his roguery, especially as it expressed itself to elderly women who had money, his terror of small children, his seemingly complete disdain for whether or not the audience appreciated or even heard his lines, all of these and many more added up to an unusual comedian.

The *New York Post* commented: "Mr. Fields' jokes were unfortunately not always new jokes. But some of the old ones seemed to wear well."

Walter Catlett, another Ziegfeld comedian, explained an act which was used in one of the *Follies* as follows:

It was a tennis act. We took turns being straight man. It was a very funny act. Bill later assembled a croquet act that was very much like it. We minced around emphasizing the dainty aspects of the game at it was played at polite upper-class parties of that time. Occasionally we'd have elegant little arguments but allow people to understand that we'd really like to break each other's necks.

Bill insisted on juggling now and then, though it didn't seem to fit into the act. Nobody could argue with him. He'd just pull up when the notion suited him and juggle until he got tired, then would go on with the act. He finally conceived the idea of batting all the balls out into the audience when we finished. It was a popular windup, but at the end of the first week Ziegfeld docked Bill's salary $86 for tennis balls.

Bill stormed in and raised the devil but Ziegfeld was firm. He said, "Your contract states that you must furnish your own props."

Mack Sennett, the famous comedy director of the early film days, who brought Fields to Hollywood, tells this anecdote:

Fields had an extra special bout with his gin bottle that night and arrived late for work the next morning. His expensive automobile was out of whack, so he came by streetcar trying to hold a newspaper in his twitching hands, while the rocking and swaying with the trolley made him weaker and sicker.

Now, there was a girl named Dora who worked for us. She boarded the streetcar and sat down by Fields, placing a small wicker basket between them. As always, the Sennett studio was amply populated with critters — we had raccoons, wolves, eagles, chickens, vermints and snakes. Dora was our snake charmer. The wicker contained a three-foot king snake.

As Mr. Fields tried to concentrate on his *Examiner,* the snake slithered out of the basket, propped itself behind Fields, and peered over his shoulder.

"It cannot be," said Mr. Fields. "It does not happen. This, of course, is a damnable illusion, a mere figment of the gin-inspired cerebellum. I shall, I will, be brave."

He reached up and stroked the king snake's brow.

Opposite page:

W. C. Fields' famous role as a cardsharp won him laughs throughout his extraordinary career.

In the movie *David Copperfield* the Mr. Micawber of W. C. Fields was more Fields than Dickens. But almost everyone agreed that Charles Dickens would have approved.

On one occasion Fields is reported to have explained to a young lady of his acquaintance that the way he had acquired his red nose was by "bruising it on a cocktail glass in his extreme youth."

On another occasion, Fields sauntered into a hotel carrying his gold-headed cane. His step was jaunty and his hat was slightly dented and frayed. At the desk, Fields rapped in typical fashion and demanded "the bridal suite."

Not recognizing the bland visage, the manager looked at Fields with some degree of fright and informed him that the bridal suite was usually reserved for gentlemen with brides.

"That is all right," the comedian answered. "I'll pick up one in town."

Once, Fields found himself in a strange town without companionship. He thereupon started out in search of entertainment. According to the story he roamed the streets until he saw a lot of vehicles lined up in front of a big house.

"I went up to the door and a butler or somebody stuck a silver plate under my nose. I put an old laundry check and a dime on it and went on in. It was a very enjoyable function. I had a long talk with the Governor's wife."

"What did you talk about, Bill?" he was asked.

"We talked about the mating habits of the Wallaby."

Eddie Cantor came to the *Follies* in 1917. As he recalls it, "When I was with the juggling act, Fanny Brice was already a star. You see, Ziegfeld had the ability to engage the best in each particular field. The best roughhouse comic in the world, without a doubt, was W. C. Fields. The best comedienne, Fanny Brice. The best comedian, Bert Williams, and I guess I had the biggest eyes so Flo hired me."

Eddie Cantor began his career as a singing waiter and learned to blacken his face with burnt cork in an attempt to change his act when breaking into vaudeville. Not a singer, not a dancer, not even a comedian, Eddie Cantor was a bundle of nerves in blackface. It was in this role in 1916 that Ziegfeld saw him playing in the musical comedy *Canary Cottage*. He recruited him into the *Follies* where he played and starred in 1917, 1918, and 1919.

The Cantor brand of humor is not so much to captivate you by wit or to win

Eddie Cantor started as a singing waiter. He has brought fun and laughter to more people during his long career than can possibly be counted.

laughter by the incongruous. Rather Cantor tends to overwhelm you by his sheer nervous energy, his prancing up and down. Occasionally he wins laughs by playing the role of the weakling in the hands of more powerful forces such as the osteopath who kneads his weak limbs like an India rubber doll. Cantor himself describes one of his typical comic scenes in *Kid Boots*.

The situation revolved about a championship golf match to be played by the rivals for Polly's hand and heart. I was trying to help Tom, the hero, get into the match and the only way was to incapacitate his friend Valentine, who had been selected by the club to represent it.

For more than five minutes I stood behind the counter with a hammer, poising it over Valentine at various times as if to crown him and make way for Tom. The comedy was primarily one of action and stage business. As I got into position for the attack, with the hammer behind my back, I inquired of Valentine, "If you were sick tomorrow you couldn't play, could you?"

"I should say not."

"How do you feel?"

"Why, I feel all right."

"I was just thinking, if anything happened to you, Tom would take your place — "

"Yes, of course, Tom is my logical successor."

"He'd take your place?"

Valentine lit a cigarette and I covered my eyes while lifting the hammer to strike him. But I weakened.

"Even — even if you had a sprained wrist you couldn't play?"

"No! The slightest thing would incapacitate me."

I wiped my brow, lifted two hammers, but hesitated again.

"Do you know anything about the law?" I suddenly inquired.

"I studied law — I'm a lawyer."

"Oh, you're a lawyer!" I put down both hammers. "I guess you could tell me what is assault?"

"Assault and battery?"

"I know what a battery is. I mean just plain assault."

"If one person strikes another with intent to injure, that is assault."

"But if it's an accident?"

"Oh, well, if it's really an accident, then the person can't be punished."

"He can't be punished?" I asked eagerly.

"No."

"Umph! That's a good law." I lifted the hammer with renewed confidence. "You feel all right?"

"I feel splendid."

"But if you had an injured wrist — zowie —the match would be off."

"But — zowie — I haven't an injured wrist."

"Ah, but you have an injured wrist." I dropped the hammer on his hand and he let out a yell that rocked the caddie shop. "Gosh! What an accident."

During the depression of the 1930's Cantor's special humor went something like this.

My throat is cut from ear to ear. I am bleeding profusely in seven other places. There is a knocking in the back of my head, my hands tremble violently, I have sharp shooting pains all over my body, and in addition to all that my general health is none too good.

One of the greatest diagnosticians in America thumped me and probed me all over the premises.

"You are a very sick man!" he said finally. "A very sick man. You are suffering from

Al Shean and Ed Gallagher sky-rocketed to fame largely as a result of their *Follies* song which included the final tagline: "Positively, Mr. Gallagher? Absolutely, Mr. Shean." Such is fame in the entertainment business.

Montgomery Ward of the liver; General Electric of the stomach; Westinghouse of the brain, and besides you have a severe case of internal combustion."

The joke's on the doctor. He didn't notice me as I walked into his office or he'd have discovered that I also had a bad limp from taking an unexpected ride in Otis Elevator. They let me in on the top floor. When I ran out of collateral, the cable snapped and I landed in the basement without a shock absorber. They sent a margin clerk and two other internes to collect the pieces.

You can readily guess that I was in the market. Brother, I wasn't *in* the market; I was *under* it. Just mention Wall Street and I'm ready to break down on your shoulder and give you a tear-drenched lapel to take home to the wife and kiddies. That is, if your broker didn't sell them at the market.

Only one fellow I know got a lucky break in this panic. That was my uncle. He died in September, B.C. — Before the Crash. Poor fellow! He had a blood pressure of 160 and when it reached 250 he tried to split it four for one.

But while the Follies were at their height in New York City, in the faraway village of Hollywood something was happening that would change the entertainment world almost overnight.

7

Flickers: from Custard Pie to Cheesecake

May Irwin, popular comedienne of the legitimate stage, participated in the making of one of the first movies with John C. Rice in a scene entitled "The Kiss." The episode was taken from the climax of their play, *The Widow Jones,* which was playing on Broadway in 1896. Above is a view of the early movie machine, the Kinetoscope, which was a sensation in its day.

At the exact moment that Flo Ziegfeld was capturing the attention of Broadway, across the country another showman of genius was presenting a somewhat smilar approach to girls and gags.

His name was Mack Sennett and he was what might be called the poor man's Ziegfeld.

Sennett operated in a different medium: the early motion pictures. He slanted his films to a different audience: the masses of people rather than the select few who could afford *Follies* ticket prices. But the two men had much in common. Both took clothes off their women and hung a reputation around the names of their comedians. But each did this in his own special way.

When moving pictures began commercially back in 1905, they were patronizingly referred to as the "flickers" or the "tape," and everybody who knew anything realized that they were but a passing fad . . . like the horseless carriage.

But of course moving pictures became an accepted theatrical medium which reflected the growing search on the part of large groups of people for inexpensive entertainment. Motion pictures represented the coming of the industrial revolution to the entertainment world.

The first great comic in the infant film industry was John Bunny, who came from the legitimate theater to the Vitagraph motion picture company when it was located in Brooklyn. Bunny was a huge, happy-looking man with a genius for comic pantomime.

"I didn't want to be a comedian," he said, "but nature was agin' me. How could I expect to play Romeo with a figure like mine? It was many years before I learned to yield gracefully to the fate for which nature had endowed me.

"I struggled along trying to make managers give me serious parts. I could do them, too. Once in Chicago I did a sob scene in the middle of a comic opera that made everybody cry. They didn't cry from self-sympathy, either. Which proves my contention that it is easier to make people cry than to make them laugh."

Bunny was a comedian in the tradition of a Charles Dickens comic character. But the infant motion-picture industry was destined to be swept into another kind of traditional comedy which featured the physical slapstick of the early buffoon, the throwing of pies and the downfall of dignity.

Young Mack Sennett was in New York seeking employment in the theater when he heard that professionals might hope to receive as high as $5 a day in the movies. At that time he was playing the hind end of a horse, and consequently he decided that the movies might be a step forward in his career. Sennett was brought to Hollywood from New York by D. W. Griffith as part of a company including Mary Pickford, Henry B. Walthall, and Owen Moore.

Early in his career, Sennett discovered that he had the knack of recognizing almost instinctively what would make an audience laugh. When a gag failed to make Mack laugh it usually was not funny to others.

From a small-bit actor Sennett shifted to directing comedies for the Keystone Film company which he founded.

Sennett was not the only or even the first pioneer in the production of American comedy films. Al Christie produced the first Hollywood film comedy in 1911 and later became the nearest competitor Mack Sennett ever had. Hal Roach, a former movie stunt man and bit player, took to producing comedies in this period and became one of the most successful in the business.

But Sennett actually had little competition when it came to new techniques for laughter. He reinvented slapstick, adding new tricks — especially breathtaking speed and pace.

89

Technicians of the custard pie soon found that there was nothing funny about a pie which half missed its target. Either the pie "mooned" its object or there was no laugh. Picture above shows Mabel Normand, first among the pie throwers, in a pie-tossing scene from *A Misplaced Foot* or *Revenge with a Pie*.

The major Sennett techniques were simple: first, pie throwing; second, the chase, usually featuring the Keystone Cops; and third, bathing beauties.

The making of a Keystone comedy was a free-wheeling operation with a minimum of script or scenario and a maximum of improvising. Directors and players were free to ad lib as they chose as long as additional expense was not involved. It was quite a commonplace for several comedians and a cameraman to go off early in the morning in search of incidents for a movie. Whether the scene was a crowded dance hall, a burning building or a runaway horse and wagon, somehow the adventuring comedians managed to turn it into successful slapstick. Such films were made at the rate of one a week.

It was the time of Roscoe (Fatty) Arbuckle, Hank Mann, Chester Conklin, and Ford Sterling. They were superb comedians by instinct. The humor was physical and robust. They had no expensive props, no big budgets, no elaborate sets; the scripts were very apt to be written down on someone's cuffs, though Mack Sennett has confessed to writing scripts eight or nine pages long. The scripts were usually torn up halfway through.

The theme of all the Keystone comedies — altogether there were about nine hundred of them — was simplicity itself.

The custard pie was one of the good old reliable laugh-getting techniques which Sennett comedies employed. Credit for throwing the first pie is frequently attributed to Sennett's great comedienne, Mabel Normand. The story goes that a director was vainly trying to make Ben Turpin, the cross-eyed wonder, loosen up and laugh. The cameras were grinding and the director was pleading.

Mabel Normand was sitting on the sidelines watching. She also observed that several workmen were eating their lunch nearby and that they had a luscious lemon pie by their side.

Mabel was a girl of many talents including a devilish sense of humor. On this occasion she simply walked over, picked up the pie, took aim, and let it go in the direction of Ben Turpin. It struck the bull's eye or, rather, Ben's eye.

In the meantime the camera had been cranking and it recorded the immortal event. Sennett, who had been sitting dourly watching the production, was noticed to be laughing uproariously — always a significant sign. When the film was developed, it was found to appear even funnier than it had at the time.

Mack Sennett's fun factory in Los Angeles.

The motion-picture audience also appeared to find pie throwing amusing. From that day on the thrown custard pie ranked high in the arsenal of Sennett comedy tricks.

Although the custard pie became part of the accepted routine of the comedies of the day, the pies were seldom actually made of custard. It was found that insects tended to settle in numbers on custard pies. Fastidious patrons of the early motion pictures did not like the idea of seeing large flies crawling over the pies before they were thrown. It seemed that pies made of blackberries not only photographed better than custard but also were free from the nuisance of photogenic flies. Furthermore, whipped-up soap lather did much better than cream.

There was also a technique to pie throwing. In his entertaining book, *King of Comedy*, Mack Sennett recalls the experience of one of the first pie-throwers: "Arbuckle was ambidextrous and had double vision like a T-formation quarterback. He could throw two pies at once in different directions." In giving directions on the throwing of a pie, one expert described it: "Actually you don't throw like a short-stop rifling to first base. You push the pie towards the face, leaving it to your follow-through. Six or eight feet is the limit for an artistic performance."

" 'Nice people' thought that pie-throwing was vulgar and that it was outrageous to laugh at such elemental humor," states Rob Wagner, former publicity man for Mack Sennett; yet there is "something fundamentally funny in seeing a body's face projected through the soft goo of a custard pie."

If the pie became standard comic technique in the Keystone comedy, so also were the Keystone cops and the chase which, more likely than not, ended a Keystone comedy. Mack Sennett started every new man as a Keystone cop to see how he worked

There were certain stock situations in the early Sennett films that were always good for a laugh. Above left is the dramatic ending of the race between Keystone Cops and a train. Below left is a scene from *Barney Oldfield's Race for Life* featuring a trio of film greats: Mack Sennett is at the legs; Ford Sterling is applying the mallet; and Mabel Normand, of course, is resting on the tracks. Below, a platoon of Keystone Cops with Sterling at the phone and Fatty Arbuckle first in line.

93

out. The cops were a harum-scarum police force who were forever careening madly down roads in zigzagging motorcars with policemen falling off the patrol wagon and climbing aboard again. Keystone cops took quite a beating in their daily antics and had to know how to fall, how to receive blows without flinching. They were a cross between an acrobat and an imbecile.

"No matter what they did," wrote Richard Watts, Jr., film critic at the time, "from vigorous tumbling to receiving berry pies in the face, the Keystone Cops achieved definite pantomimic effects not like those of stage clowns in their antics but reacting to an entirely new medium."

The third major innovation that Sennett brought to the films was the bathing beauty. It all came about through the efforts of Sennett's publicity men to obtain more attention from the daily newspapers for the Keystone productions. It was discovered that the actors and actresses engaged in comic roles were not receiving the notice that they thought they should receive from the press.

When it came to the attention of Sennett that there always appeared to be space in the press for pretty girls, particularly if their knees were showing, he summoned

Ford Sterling was tops in comedians under Sennett and enjoyed great popularity until Chaplin entered the scene.

The lot of a slapstick comedian was not an easy one. Falls from moving vehicles, wild auto rides, races with trains, duckings in ponds, being targets for pies, rocks and sacks of flour, were all in a day's work. But there were redeeming moments, too. At right is Mack Swain, a comic reliable, pictured with a then-unknown Sennett bathing beauty, Gloria Swanson.

his staff and said, as he describes it, "Boys, take a look at this. This is how to get our pictures in the paper. Go hire some girls, any girls, so long as they're pretty, especially around the knees." The results evidently proved satisfactory because the Sennett productions obtained more space in the newspapers. One step, however, was to lead to another. The next move was to use the beautiful girls collected for publicity purposes in the movies themselves.

Said Sennett, "Sure, we know they can't act. But they don't have to act. Put them in bathing suits and just have them around to be looked at while the comics are making funny." Of course, this was not exactly an innovation since Sennett had learned in burlesque and knew what attraction a pretty girl could have on the stage, especially if she was not dressed for sub-zero weather.

Sennett did not present his bathing beauties without sharp opposition, particularly when he designed new bathing suits the like of which had not been seen before. One biographer of Sennett says that "Mack's abbreviations were always an inch or two shorter than the prevailing bathing styles . . . nor did he realize that his pictures seen by millions of women were, in effect, an emancipation proclamation. He simply

Moviegoers roared at the antics of the early film clowns. Among the brightest personalities were Larry Semon and Al St. John (top row); Ben Turpin and Clyde Cook (second
row); Slim Summerville and Mack Swain (bottom row).

was giving his audience what they wanted. And he did more in a few years to free the women of America from their horse blanket pagodas than had any other man or woman in centuries of editorializing."

The Mack Sennett comedies continued to be churned out, most of them one-reelers, jumpy and jerky, full of unrelated incidents, violent slugging Keystone cops, pie-throwing comics, self-conscious bathing beauties, no plot, little story, repetitious gags. But despite all the weaknesses, they provided a welcome relief for the entertainment-seeking public.

The comedies were something for the common people at last. They gave dignity and authority a swift kick in the pants or a mushy pie in the face, and got away with it. They were the answer to the common man's dream. So were the pretty girls. Small wonder that Mack Sennett films became favorites from one end of the nation to the other. Of course, the stars that Sennett developed had something to do with this, too. The roster of the people that passed through the Sennett studios in the early days included Charlie Chaplin, Gloria Swanson, Buster Keaton, Carole Lombard, Marie Dressler, Polly Moran, W. C. Fields, Bing Crosby, Ford Sterling, Charlie Murray, Hank Mann, Harry Langdon, Phyllis Haver, Marie Prevost, Mabel Normand, Slim Summerville, Fatty Arbuckle and scores more.

Chester Conklin and his walrus mustache were known everywhere by lovers of the early movies. Here Chester is pictured with four typical Mack Sennett bathing beauties.

Among his women stars, Mack Sennett rated Mabel Normand as tops. "Mabel Normand could do everything that Chaplin could do," he said. "To me, she was the greatest comedian that ever lived."

Sennett was not the only one who considered Mabel one of the most talented and capable comediennes in all movie history. Marie Dressler, herself a star of major magnitude on stage and screen, recalls Mabel:

I wish I could make you see her as I remember her. Dark, little, vivaciously pretty, as active and as mischievous as a monkey, she was the first great comedienne of the screen. Always willing to risk life and limb to give the fans a thrill, she used to spend half of her time laid up in a hospital for repairs.

She was an artist's model in New York when Mack Sennett discovered her and gave her a chance in the films. Mabel kept the Keystone lot in gales of laughter, and as a natural wit and tease, she adored plaguing us all. Some of her bon mots are still current in Hollywood.

Even when Mabel Normand gained stardom she would not permit herself to be pampered. She would permit of no "double" for her hazardous rides, leaps or falls.

Mack Sennett was an innovator. He gave his stars custard pies, but wouldn't let them eat them. He put his girls in bathing suits, but wouldn't let them swim in them.

Max Linder, a French comedian who made films in this country, contributed inspiration to the early careers of many silent screen laugh makers.

When a doctor advised her not to take chances with her health and safety, she said: "What in hell's the difference, if it makes a lot of people laugh?"

One of the mainstays of the Mack Sennett productions was Ford Sterling, the first Keystone cop and one of the most popular comedians on the screen. Sterling was rated among the very top three of the comedians, his closest rivals being John Bunny and Max Linder, the French comedian. Sterling had been a clown in the circus and had played all over the country with small stock companies. He was a comedian of a muscular type who fitted in with the hard chores which made up the slapstick comedy of the day. With him were Fatty Arbuckle in the 300-lb. class, and Doc Swain of nearly similar weight who could endure the hardships, the falls, the tumbles, the pie-throwing, pie-receiving antics which went into the daily lot of the Mack Sennett slapsticks.

Scarcely anyone would have believed that within a short space of time a slightly built, timid young man was to replace huge Ford Sterling as chief comedian of the Sennett films and sky-rocket to become one of the greatest comedians in the history of the world.

Charlie Chaplin to Mickey Mouse

Mack Sennett had a good eye for figures but a poor memory for names. When it came to recalling that young British comic whom he had seen in New York in the play *Mumming Birds* the best he could do was to recall that the name began with a C. Perhaps it was Chambort or Chadwick.

But whether he remembered the name of the young comic or not, Sennett was shrewd enough to recognize talent when he saw it. At the time, Sennett commented to Mabel Normand, "Mabel, if there's one thing I can do it's to spot talent. Why I didn't think of this fellow before is beyond me. Maybe because Sterling, Arbuckle and the rest have gone ahead so fast. But this chap, what's his name, Carlson or Kinkaid, has got something."

"He was funny," admitted Mabel Normand, "there was something kind of sad about him. That's what I remembered most. He was sad; he made your heart ache, but he was funny. Don't you remember I said, 'That guy was born with strikes on him'? What was his name, anyway?"

Sennett telegraphed his agent and described the man that he wanted in detail. There was a delay before he received a telegram.

FELLOW'S NAME CHARLIE CHAPLIN STOP HAS FORTY WEEKS
SOLID BOOKING STOP WON'T TAKE CHANCE WITH MOVIES

Sennett replied urging his agent to find out what Chaplin was earning on the stage and to offer him three times his salary. Chaplin was then receiving $40 a week. His agent promised him $125 to sign with Keystone. Chaplin agreed.

The pantomime vaudeville troupe that he was playing with was in Philadelphia at the time. Chaplin signed a contract in the late summer of 1913.

The deal was done but Sennett had grave misgivings about the possibilities of his new employee. He actually had never seen him offstage, did not know how he would photograph or whether his type of humor would be fitting for the screen.

"When I got the contract," Charlie recalls, "I immediately began to attend every picture show where Keystone comedies were being shown. I was terror-struck! I saw Mabel Normand leaping about on the edges of high buildings, jumping from bridges, doing all manner of falls. If they expected that of a woman what would they expect of me?"

When Charlie presented himself to Sennett's Hollywood studio the doorman stopped him at the gate, refusing him entrance until he was rescued by Mack Sennett himself.

As Mack Sennett recalls it, it was days and days before Charlie Chaplin put over anything real. "He tried all sorts of make-ups — one of them, I remember, was a fat man — but they were all about equally flat. The fact of it was that for some time I felt a little uneasy as to whether my find was a very fortunate one."

Comedians helped the sale of Liberty Bonds during World War I. Front row are Marie Dressler and Charlie Chaplin. Standing, left to right, Franklin D. Roosevelt the Under Secretary of the Navy, Douglas Fairbanks and Mary Pickford.

Joseph Grimaldi, British panto-mime clown, influenced the de-velopment of Charlie Chaplin's type of humor. When the talkies came, Chaplin said that they "come to ruin the world's most ancient art, the art of panto-mime."

Chaplin himself says:

I was a tramp at the beginning and they wanted me to do all the usual slapstick stunts. I had to beg them to let me play the part my way. "If you want somebody to pull all the old gags," I said to Sennett, "why did you hire me? You get a man at $25 to do this sort of stuff!" So at last they gave in to my idea. This I had worked out very carefully; a tramp in a fine hotel — there's a universal situation for you. Hardly a human being hasn't duplicated the feeling of being alone, poor, out of touch with the gay crowd about him, of trying to identify himself somehow with the fine alien throng. So I did the little touches here of imi-tation — the pulling down of shabby cuffs, the straightening of my hat, all the gestures that gave a wider meaning to the characterization.

Mabel Normand recalls, "They didn't really appreciate Charlie in those early days. I remember numerous times when people at the studio came up and asked me confidentially, 'Say, do you think he's so funny? In my mind he can't touch Ford Sterling.' They were just so used to slapstick that imaginative comedy couldn't penetrate."

The story has often been told of how Chaplin came to adopt the costume for which he became famous. There are many stories, some true, some not quite so true. Actually a picture of the Charlie Chaplin character had been in Charlie's mind for a long time. It had come out of his studies of London street types. He took Mack Swain's mustache, in abbreviated style. He wore Ford Sterling's immense trousers, and took his huge shoes and wore them on the wrong feet. Actually, Chaplin did more than borrow Ford's shoes. Both figuratively and literally Chaplin filled Ster-ling's shoes and it was only a short time before Sterling left Sennett's employ to seek work elsewhere. Chaplin had supplanted Sterling as the Number One clown of the Sennett organization, and Sterling was never to recover his former laurels.

From the start it was acknowledged that Chaplin would be the sole exception to the custard-pie, Keystone-cop, bathing-beauty routine which was the regular formula for all other Sennett comedians. While Chaplin participated somewhat in this routine and actually played a Keystone cop early in his career, he seldom took part in the full formula because it was clear nearly from the outset that Chaplin had his own type of artistry.

This artistry was to result in a wave of popularity for the Chaplin brand of comedy which swept the nation. Just fourteen months after he had timidly arrived in Hollywood as an employee of Mack Sennett at $125 a week, Chaplin left the Sennett Studio to join the Essanay film-making company for $1,250 a week. The following year, 1916, Chaplin was making $10,000 a week and a bonus of $150,000 when he signed with the Mutual Film Corporation. And the year after that, Chaplin was earning no less than $1,075,000 for eight two-reel pictures with the First National Exhibitors Circuit.

In an interview in this early period, Chaplin remarked that it only took about two weeks' work at the Keystone plant to make him very enthusiastic about pictures, especially farces.

I study the screen closely now, and I am firmly convinced that everyone in the industry should do likewise. There are many things that we can learn from it, even though we think we have perfected ourselves in our own line of the great industry.

I endeavor to put nothing in my farces which is not a burlesque on something in real life. No matter how senseless a thing may seem on the screen, I think that if it is studied carefully it can be traced back to life, and is probably an everyday occurrence which the would-be critic of the farce had thought to be a bit funny.

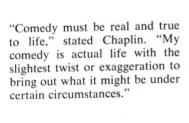

"Comedy must be real and true to life," stated Chaplin. "My comedy is actual life with the slightest twist or exaggeration to bring out what it might be under certain circumstances."

A typical Chaplin film gem is *Shoulder Arms*. Here's how Theodore Huff, Chaplin biographer, describes it:

In the first scene Charlie is a member of the "awkward squad" in a training camp. We see him at drill and the sergeant ordering "Put those feet in!" Trying to obey the drill commands, Charlie tangles himself up as the rest of the squad march off. He catches up with the others, to go into a sequence of in-turning and out-turning of his toes accompanied by barked commands. At dismissal Charlie hops to his tent to fall exhausted on his cot (fade out).

"Over there." Charlie staggers in under knapsacks, rifle, blankets, household utensils, etc. Tapping an officer on the shoulder for directions, he walks forward (moving camera) to a sign labeled: *Broadway and Rotten Row*. The new recruit is put through an inspection by a sergeant who gets his fingers caught in provident Charlie's rat trap. With his billowing equipment he gets stuck in the dugout door and is helped through, finally, by a boot from the sergeant. His first act, when he reaches his quarters, is to hang up a nutmeg grater to scratch his back on, the "cooties" having already "occupied" him.

The scene shifts to the enemy trenches where a pint-size, goose-stepping German officer carries on an inspection, consisting mainly of kicks. Back in Charlie's trench, he and the sergeant enjoy a "quiet lunch" during the shelling. Charlie is told to make himself at home as his helmet bounces around with the detonations.

Later Charlie is standing guard in pouring rain, dreaming of home. In a split screen effect we see, on the left, a New York street scene dissolving to a bartender serving drinks. As Charlie smiles, the vision fades back to the muddy trench. The guard is changed, and the miserable soldier marches to his bed and lies down — all in rhythm.

A postman brings "news from home." Charlie rushes forward, only to hear everybody's name called but his own. Sitting on his bunk, he leans disconsolately on his elbow. As Sid and another soldier open food packages, Charlie, refusing snacks offered by his buddies, nibbles the cheese in his trap. Sauntering outside, moodily he looks over the shoulder of a man reading a letter and reacts vicariously as if it were his own, smiling when the other man smiles, or registering concern. He leans forward for a closer look, smiles again — until the soldier glares and moves away.

The mailman returns. "This must be yours." Charlie frantically opens his package — to

When Chaplin first came to the Sennett studio he shared the dressing room with the oversize 300-pound Roscoe "Fatty" Arbuckle, a popular favorite. Alongside of giants Arbuckle and Mack Swain, Chaplin appeared almost insignificant.

Chaplin and Ford Sterling were rivals in real life as well as on the screen as in top pix, left. Right, top, Chaplin in *The Immigrant*. Lower left, Chaplin and Jackie Coogan in *The Kid*. Lower right, Chaplin in *Shoulder Arms*. This page, upper, Harold Lloyd on the bottom in a scene from "The Freshman." Right, Chaplin, the musician, composed the score for most of his later films.

Charlie Chaplin, Cheerful Comedian

Though this title tells little,
of a doubt, is the funniest man
asserted, without coming far fro
There remains little to be sa

FOUR MORE DAYS LEFT FOR CHAPLIN CONTEST

By this time all of you who have applied must have your back copies of last week's Evening Journal for the Charlie Chaplin contest. You have until Saturday midnight to send them in—four more days.

You can thank the extraordinary success of the contest for your

erly assembled, on a blank sheet of paper so that they form a com-

Isn't Chap

THE curiously assorted bill at the
hardly more

New Stunt---Imitating a Popular Film Player

STAGE ENTRANCE

CHAPLIN CONTEST TO-NIGHT

Callahan

More Than Thirty Picture Houses Have Amateur Chaplin Nights.   Here Are Some of the Amateurs.

The Real Charlie Chaplin
The Personal Side of the Famous Comedian as His Associates Know

Why Is Charlie Chaplin?

The Chaplin craze swept the nation. Clippings give a brief indication of the variety of newspaper notices. Chaplin was seldom satisfied with his own perfomances. "It's a desperate business being a clown," he once said.

extract a dog biscuit and Limberger cheese. Protecting himself with a gas mask he tosses the cheese like a grenade across No Man's Land into the enemy trenches. It lands on the face of the little German officer just as he is toasting their early arrival in Paris.

"Bedtime" finds the little dugout half filled with water. Only the sergeant's head and his feet, with a frog perched on one of them, shows above the water. Charlie lifts his pillow out of the water, to fluff it before he lies down, then pulls the sopping blanket over him. The sergeant's snoring is so effective that when Charlie scoops water over to his open mouth, a geyser results. Splashing back at him, the sergeant orders him to "Stop rocking the boat!" A lighted candle comes floating by and Charlie blows it, like a little sailboat, toward Sid's protruding toes, and plays innocent when the hot-footed man awakes. Charlie hunts a more comfortable spot at the other end of the bunk only to have his head submerge. With the help of a phonograph horn as a breathing tube, he settles down to a submarine snooze.

As zero hour approaches next morning Charlie finds that his identification tag is number 13. Pulling a mirror out of his pocket he primps as a means of bracing his courage. Ordered "over the top," Charlie rushes heroically up the ladder which hurtles back into the mud. "13 is not so unlucky."

He is next seen herding a line of captured Germans, among them the little officer, whom Charlie takes on his lap for a spanking. This earns him the admiration of a huge German soldier, who shakes his head. Asked how he captured them, Charlie makes the now classic reply, "I surrounded them."

With the tremendous interest in Chaplin films came a wave of Chaplinism which spread to every corner of the nation as well as the world itself. Theaters held amateur contests for Chaplin imitations. Many a comedian got by solely on his ability to imitate Chaplin. There was scarcely a child in the United States at the time who hadn't at some point taken a cane, painted on a false mustache, and walked across the room imitating Chaplin.

As Bob Hope recalls, "Charlie Chaplin imitations had made me show-business conscious. I'd put on my Chaplin make-up and walk duck-legged down to the corner past the firehouse. I twirled a rattan cane and wore flapping, oversized battered shoes. Amateur Charlie Chaplin contests had broken out in the country's theaters like a rash. I was so good at it that I was persuaded to enter a contest at Luna Park. To make sure I won, my brothers rounded up all the neighborhood kids to vote for me."

Milton Berle got his start as a Chaplin impersonator. Ben Blue's first job, at the age of thirteen, was doing imitations of Chaplin, acting as a "shill" to ballyhoo the latest Chaplin picture.

The influence of Charlie Chaplin in the world of comedy can hardly be exaggerated. The new medium of motion pictures was thirsting for popular heroes, sufficiently sensitive to appeal to the people's hearts and native sense of humor which is always so close to the tragic. Chaplin's talents and sympathies lent themselves admirably to satisfy this need. But he was by no means the only major figure in the laugh-making business of the early silent films.

The fact was that motion-pictures for the first time gave to entertainers an audience of millions. People were learning to frequent the motion picture theater as a means of entertainment, and comedy was their favorite. Jack Bunny, Mack Sennett, Charlie Chaplin were among the first pioneers in movie laugh making. But they were to be challenged for top laurels by an ever-increasing number of fun-

Harold Lloyd was the only comedian to rival Chaplin as a box-office attraction. Lloyd (left) at height of his career. Right with Wally Howe, examining the original Harold Lloyd spectacles.

nymen who were to set new marks of popularity of their own. Among the first of these challengers for the title, whose box-office accomplishments even surpassed Chaplin in certain peak years, was Harold Lloyd. He was to open the way for a parade of popular film comedians whose names helped make Hollywood into a golden Mecca for film folks.

Like many other laugh makers, Harold Lloyd at first found it difficult to resist the Chaplin influence no matter how hard he tried. In his early characters of Willie Work and Lonesome Luke, he attempted to select characters at the opposite poles from Chaplin but found that the Chaplin influence was so great that he was constantly accused of imitation.

Sam Goldwyn, the producer, recalls an incident involving Lloyd.

The first time I ever met Lloyd was at a dinner at which Chaplin was also present. The latter was talking on one of his favorite themes, religion or economics, I forget which, and his words, always clipped just enough to reveal his English birth, were coming thick and fast. I noticed that as he spoke, a rather tall, rather serious-looking young fellow, who was one of a group in an opposite corner of the room, was looking at him wonderingly, almost wistfully. He himself was not saying a word.

"Who is that chap over there?" I asked one of the men sitting next to me.

"Oh, don't you know him? That's Harold Lloyd, the comedian."

"Quiet fellow, isn't he?" I remarked. "I've hardly heard him say a word."

"He's usually like that at parties," replied the other man. "I've been around with the boy

Lloyd was one of the first movie comedians to use trick photography in a professional way. He would dangle by his heels, seemingly far above city streets, walk narrow girders, escape plunging to his destruction by an eyelash. Actually he was only a few feet from solid ground when such a picture as the one at left was taken.

a lot and I've never once seen him cut up like Buster Keaton or Charlie Chaplin. He says he doesn't feel that way when he isn't on the set — that it isn't until he gets on the old horn-rimmed spectacles and the rest of the make-up that his comedy catches up with him."

"What sort of a chap is he anyway?" asked I a few moments later. The answer was prompt and incisive. "The nicest, kindest, most wholesome, most sincere young fellow in Hollywood. Harold Lloyd — why he is the sort of kid you sit around and pray your daughter would marry!"

When Lloyd first came to Hollywood, he found himself rejected by the studios and even the shrewd Mack Sennett bounced him from his studio as one without ability. Hal Roach, by now a producer of successful comedy films, showed keener judgment and teamed up with Lloyd to make a series of early comic shorts.

Lloyd, however, was still in search of a comic character which was not based on the Chaplin tradition and which would be funny in its own right. As Lloyd himself describes it:

I had been feeling around for a youth, possibly a boy, who could be carried through a college series — a comedy Frank Merriwell — for a long time when I saw a dramatic picture in a downtown theatre. The central character was a fighting parson, tolerant and peaceful until riled, then a Tartar. Glasses emphasized his placidity.

The heavy had stolen the girl, carrying her away on horseback. The parson leaped on another horse, pursued, overtook the villain, dragged him from his horse, and the two were lost in a cloud of dust. When the dust cleared, the heavy lay prone and still while the par-

114

Harry Langdon was popular despite the fact that he usually seemed on the verge of tears. With his baby face and childlike innocence, he was a forerunner of the Gobel type of humor of more recent years.

Lloyd Hamilton was another favorite of the silent era, with his pancake hat and ducklike walk. Some believe that he influenced Jackie Gleason, at least insofar as his style of walking is concerned. "Making people laugh is harder than making them cry," Hamilton once said.

You might not guess the identity of any of the three above unless you were a confirmed moviegoer of several decades ago. Left to right, Chester Conklin; Leo, the walking lion; and W. C. Fields in *Tillie's Punctured Romance*.

son dusted his clothes with careless flecks of his handkerchief, replaced his glasses and resumed his ministerial calm.

I did not feel cut out for a fighting parson, but the basic idea was there . . . the glasses would serve as my trademark and at the same time suggest the character — quiet, normal, boyish, clean, sympathetic, not impossible to romance. I would need no eccentric make-up, "mull," or funny clothes. I would be an average recognized American youth and let the situation take care of the comedy.

The comedy should be better for not depending on a putty nose or its equivalent. The situation should be better for not being tied to low-comedy coattails; funnier things happen in life to an ordinary boy than to a Lonesome Luke.

There is more magic in a pair of horn-rimmed glasses than the opticians dream of, nor did I guess the half of it when I put them on in 1917.

With them, I am Harold Lloyd; without them, a private citizen. I can stroll unrecognized down any street in the land at any time without the glasses, a boon granted to no other picture star and one which some of them would pay well for. At a cost of seventy-five cents they provide a trademark recognized instantly wherever pictures are shown. They make low-comedy clothes unnecessary, permit enough romantic appeal to catch the feminine eye, usually averted from comedies, and they hold me down to no particular type or range of story.

It was chance that they are horn-rimmed. The parson's glasses in the dramatic picture that inspired them were not tortoise shells, but when I came to choose a pair of my own the vogue of horn rims was new and it was youth, principally, that was adopting them. The novelty was a picture asset and the suggestion of youth fitted perfectly with the character I had in mind.

We took out the lenses immediately, knowing that the reflection of light on the glass would be troublesome. The first pair, bought out of stock, were too heavy; the second pair had so large a diameter that the rims covered my eyebrows and killed a great deal of expression. A third pair that just suited was found in a little optical shop in Spring Street, after scouring Los Angeles. I remember hunting through a tray containing probably thirty pairs before coming on the right one. I wore them for a year and a half, guarding them with my life. When the frame broke from wear and tear I went on patching it with everything, from paste to spirit gum, for three months, until progressive dissolution forced us to send them East to an optical-goods manufacturer for duplication.

The young man on the right may look familiar. Starting from the left: Buster Keaton, Polly Moran and, you've guessed it, Jimmy Durante in the silent movie *Her Cardboard Lover*. Behind his great stone face, Keaton was a keen student of comedy. "The best way to get a laugh," he said, "is to create a genuine thrill and then relieve the tension with comedy."

Another comedian who was a formidable rival for the "funniest" was Buster Keaton, the "great stone face" of the silent era.

Keaton entered the entertainment business at the age of three when he accompanied his mother and father on the stage as one of "The Three Keatons." When the early movies were in the market for comedy types, Keaton applied and became one of Mack Sennett's many finds.

Keaton, like Harold Lloyd, had need of establishing some character type which he soon discovered to be a blank, expressionless face — as devoid of human emotion as a dishpan. Some insist that Keaton at his prime in the 1920's was second to none in comedy. His flat top hat and his blank visage applied to hilarious comedy situations was a sure laugh maker. Roughhouse was Keaton's stock in trade, and whether thrust head foremost into a cannon or tossed from a burning building, he kept his face as composed as if sipping cocktails in a lounge.

It was only the coming of talking pictures that cut short Keaton's vast popularity. His greatest pictures included *The Saphead, The Navigator, The General* and *Steamboat Bill, Jr.*

Marie Dressler, a friend of seven Presidents, favorite of the legitimate stage of the 1880's, became a silent motion picture star late in her career. Not content with that, she teamed up with Wallace Beery to make a tremendous success of the talkie, *Min and Bill*. Marie became *Tugboat Annie* to a new generation.

Another great comedian of the period and an admirer of Chaplin was Marie Dressler. She was one of the most beloved women on the stage and, in her later life, in the movies. Marie was a personal friend or acquaintance of no fewer than seven Presidents of the United States.

"I have no vivid impressions of my meeting with Mr. Cleveland or with his successor, McKinley," said Miss Dressler, "but I recall as plainly as if it were yesterday my introduction to Theodore Roosevelt. Of all the personalities I have encountered in public or private life, his was the most vigorous and magnetic." During World War I she was a guest of Mrs. Woodrow Wilson at the Summer White House.

During the War, Marie Dressler was a favorite with the World War I G.I.'s. and one of the first detachments to land in France named a street and a cow after her. "The boys had a lot of fun with my bovine namesake," said Marie Dressler. "She gave so much rich sweet milk and cream that one company was always stealing her from another. Company A would march off one morning secure in the possession of Dressler, only to find when they returned to their billets that she was contentedly munching fodder in Company B's stable.

"One bright day I woke up to find headlines screaming 'Marie Dressler killed in line of duty.' The text beneath explained that it was the cow, not the actress, who had been felled by the enemy. Nevertheless, I had a hard time convincing people that the report of my death had been greatly exaggerated."

One amusing incident Marie Dressler liked to tell involved Will Rogers:

The Newspaper Women's Club of New York gave its annual ball at the Ritz while I lived there. I was among those present. Toward the shank of the evening, I got a note from Will Rogers begging me to come over to his table. When I presented myself, my back crawling with terror because I thought I was going to be called on to put on a stunt of some sort, I saw at once that Will was in what he would describe as a "stew." His brow was corrugated with frowns. . . .

"Look here, Muree," said Will, "I'm in a peck of trouble and you got to help me out."

"Anything I can do, Will," I assured him, meanwhile doing a little private stewing of my

Wallace Beery and Raymond Hatton played together in silent films. Here the pair move a piano. As usual, Hatton ended up carrying the entire load with Beery supervising. In the early comedy films Beery often impersonated a woman.

Stan Laurel and Oliver Hardy (upper left) were perhaps the most popular box-office attraction of their time. Lower left, Zazu Pitts had a meek and re-signed humor all her own. Right, Will Rogers seldom agreed to use make-up in his films. Rare picture shows him applying make-up to his weather-beaten visage.

own as I tried to think of something bright enough to sing or say before such a crowd. "Anything I can do — you know that."

"Well," stammered Will, mopping his face, "it ain't much, Muree. Nothin' I wouldn't do for you, if you was caught in a pinch like me."

"Out with it," I commanded, by this time prepared to walk on my hands around the Crystal Room if by so doing I could abate Will's distress.

"It's like this," poor Will went on, nervously displaying a small gold laurel wreath that lay on the table in front of him. "I'm the chairman of the committee to award this durn thing to the most beautiful woman in the room. There's so many good-looking dames here I'm scared to pick one for fear the others'll jump on me and tear my hair out by the roots. So I thought — that is, I *kinder* thought, Muree — if you'd stand there and let me put this durn thing on your head, the crowd would kinder laugh it off and nobody'd get mad!"

So — I helped Will out and nobody got mad, not even Muree. Thus I, who at the tender age of five learned that I was an ugly duckling, found myself at fifty crowned Queen of Beauty. Truly the ways of Providence are inscrutable.

Marie Dressler's career was unique. She started her career in legitimate theater, where she became an outstanding comedienne. She played with Eddie Foy in *Little Robinson Crusoe,* starred in *The Lady Slavey,* and appeared with Weber and Fields in *Higgledy-Piggledy* and *Twiddle Twaddle.* She moved into vaudeville circles and also achieved a national reputation there. While in vaudeville, she was observed by that ever-ready scout of comedy, Mack Sennett, who invited her to come to Hollywood to participate in the making of the early comedies.

Though a woman past her youth, Marie went to Hollywood and participated in the making of one of the first full-length comedy pictures, *Tillie's Punctured Romance,* with Charlie Chaplin and Mabel Normand. Incidently, the infant who appeared in this picture was Milton Berle.

Mickey Mouse, a Walt Disney creation, has been, without doubt, the most widely admired rodent in all history. While he did not succeed Chaplin as a center of attention, he did win a vast audience from people of all ages. Unlike Chaplin, Lloyd and other comedians, Mickey never seems to grow old.

Marie Dressler remained in Hollywood when the talking pictures arrived and was one of the outstanding stars of the early talking pictures.

"I was born homely," she used to say, "and for fifty years it has been my lot to make my living on the stage where the first requisite for a woman's success is supposed to be a face that's easy on the eyes. I was born serious and I have earned my bread by making other people laugh . . . when everything else fails I get my voice down to the audience and make a face."

But the new motion picture industry had not succeeded in displacing the legitimate theater. Although more people laughed at a mouse in a week than laughed at a Broadway show in many months, still the "legit" carried on. . . .

122

9

The "Legit" Carries On

It was hard to tell from the bright lights glowing along Broadway in the 1920's that the legitimate theater and vaudeville were about to suffer a crushing blow.

If you looked closely, however, you could read signs that all was not well. For instance, clauses were placed in many contracts forbidding motion-picture work. Legitimate-theater managers rubbed their chins speculatively as they noted the mounting public attendance at the movies, based considerably on their lower admission costs.

But the world of flesh-and-blood entertainment seemed boomingly well. No voice boomed louder to proclaim its health than that of Al Jolson, whose one brief encounter with the silent films had soured him temporarily on ever again leaving the legitimate theater.

Al Jolson got his start in the early 1900's as a burnt-cork singer in Lou Dockstadter's minstrel.

On the legitimate stage, Jolson was a human tornado and he took Broadway by storm. "He flings into a comic song or three-minute impersonation so much energy, violence, so much of the totality of one human being," wrote a critic of the time, "that you feel it would suffice for a hundred others."

Jolson's "you ain't heard nothin' yet" was not just a comic expression. It represented an actual attitude of Jolson's toward his audience because the man could keep himself singing, dancing and joking for as long as there were laughs available from the audience. Among his plays were *Sinbad, Bombo, Big Boy.*

As one friend described him, "When Al started to sing, he really gripped you. You couldn't move a muscle."

One night in a café he had just finished his song when a deafening burst of noise from a building project across the street drowned out the applause. At the top of his lungs, Jolson hollered, "You think that's noise! You ain't heard nothin' yet!"

Then he proceeded to deliver an encore which for sheer blasting power put to everlasting shame all the noise the carpenters, the bricklayers and the drillers were making in competition.

Al Jolson worked his way painfully to the top of his ladder, emerging as the king of show business. One critic acknowledged sheepishly, "I must admit that when Jolson gets on stage I forget all about the play's deficiencies . . . there is only one Jolson and he is a natural force as great as the Mississippi."

The secret of Jolson's attraction was in the inexhaustible supply of energy that he poured into every lyric and every movement, and his incomparable faculty for captivating the hearts of his audience. He went a long way toward making people actually believe the words, no matter how ridiculous, of the song he might be singing. Alexander Leftwich, who directed Jolson, said, "He would never save up anything for the next scene, for the next act or the next day. Even at rehearsal he could never hold back, no matter how his managers pleaded with him to save his strength. He seemed to have enough lung power for an army."

There is a story that when Jolson's talents were employed by a phonograph company to make gramophone records in the early days, Jolson found it exceedingly dif-

"Al Jolson," wrote Joe Laurie, Jr., "was the greatest of all American entertainers." Jolson proudly referred to himself as a comedian.

ficult to sit still and direct his songs right into the big horn. He could only stay still for a moment or two and then he would be up prancing about.

In desperation, the phonograph company executives hired two employees to hold him down. They tried their best but Jolson kept squirming out of their grasp. Finally, as a gag, a strait jacket was procured and the protesting Jolson was placed in it and then ordered to do his recording.

"I'm the only man in the world who recorded in a strait jacket," he later told his friends.

Jolson hated to see an audience go home. One night during a long revue he observed that some members of his company appeared to be getting tired. Confronting them he said, "All right, kids. Go home. I don't need any help." Then he tossed aside his script and did a marathon song fest of more than a dozen numbers.

Once Jolson got the feel of an audience, he violated most of the rules of the theater. For example, he would sit down at the end of the runway (previously used only in burlesque) dangling his feet over the sides, and start gossiping, joking, exchanging comments with the audience as if he were at a private party at home.

Jolson's views on comedy are important.

As everyone knows who cares to know, the life of a comedian is very hard. Most of them, I have been told, are trained in infancy. I have no training; therefore, I suppose, "it's a gift" with me. And yet, the stage manager very often reminds me that it isn't; and then I remind him that he isn't. However, early in my meteoric career, I discovered that an audience must be trained to laugh.

An audience of any kind must be made to laugh. You can't coax them, and you can't tell them that you're funny unless you make them believe it. They just hate to laugh when you want them to, and when you want them to cry, they laugh. There isn't anything on earth so obstinate and perverse as an audience. Most of them are untaught, and although my task has not been to educate them, I have sometimes felt that I should like to make them realize how happy they would be if they would only just try to laugh, just even once.

There was something about Jolson which made him top man in whatever field of entertainment he entered. He didn't have a great voice, but he was a great singer. He didn't have a clever patter of jokes, but he made people laugh. Some say it was his energy; others, his personality; but most everyone agreed he was King of Entertainers.

Another great comic was Bobby Clark, who started his long career at laugh making in a minstrel show in the early 1900's. He served as a clown in the circus, in vaudeville and then in burlesque. Clark joined with Paul McCullough and the team of Clark and McCullough became one of the most successful comedy teams in the legitimate show business.

Clark was strictly a prop man and always depended on physical antics and his famous leer to provide the laughs. His cigar, his cane and his painted-on glasses are trademarks of his humor.

The story is that as a clown in the early days he wore shell-rimmed glasses. One day he mislaid them and frantically hit upon the idea of painting on the glasses in their place. He has worn them ever since.

"I guess I'll die with them on," Clark says. "Managers won't have me otherwise."

Ed Wynn was one of the first major comedians to eliminate slapstick from his repertoire. His act was more that of sidewalk conversation. His sure laugh getters were his many inventions, such as the corn-on-the-cob typewriter carriage which would ring a bell when the eater reached the end of a line; or the use of a pair of mechanical windshield wipers for his eyeglasses when eating grapefruit. He used many labor-saving devices on the stage. Dragging a toy wagon before the footlights, he took from it a safety device for noiseless soups, or a coffee cup with a hole in the bottom (to save the labor of pouring the coffee into the saucer).

His chief prop was the use of ridiculous hats which he kept changing during the course of his performance. His father, interestingly, was in the millinery business.

Ed Wynn was a lovable buffoon with his wearing of silly hats, crazy costumes and huge shoes. He pretended to lisp in a high-pitched voice, and giggled at the slightest provocation.

He played vaudeville for many years before starring in such shows as *The Deacon and the Lady, Ziegfeld Follies, The Perfect Fool, The Grab Bag.*

Wynn was an innovator, too. He was one of the first recognized masters of ceremonies, having started back in 1913 when he was on the opening bill of the Palace Theatre, the pinnacle in American vaudeville. When something went wrong with the signs announcing the sequence of acts, Wynn convinced the manager that he should announce the acts in person. Soon jokes were added and Wynn became a part of each act on the bill. The same technique was proposed by Wynn to Ziegfeld when he played in the *Follies*. It became a standard technique for *Follies* comedians after that.

Wynn was a shrewd judge of his fellow comedians. It was he who coaxed W. C. Fields to speak lines during his juggling act when Fields was a silent *Ziegfeld Follies* comedy juggler. And again it was Wynn who convinced Will Rogers to do more than spin ropes and to add yarns to his repertoire. "Rogers was the funniest man I ever heard in private," Wynn recalls, "but he didn't dare say anything when on the stage. I urged him to try. He took the plunge and became one of the funniest comedians Ziegfeld ever had."

Later in life it was Ed Wynn who started the vogue of joshing the radio commercials. "I'll stick to my horse, Graham," he would lisp to Graham McNamee, the announcer, when he was proclaiming a gasoline commercial.

The unique characteristic of Ed Wynn has been his amazing ability to adapt his genuine comic spirit to changing conditions. His career has encompassed three or more personalities: the Rah, Rah, Rah Boy; the Boy with the Funny Hat; the King's Jester; the Perfect Fool; the Fire Chief.

A generation of radio listeners recalls the comic Ed Wynn letter-answering service as part of the Fire Chief program. So popular was this program that moving-picture houses announced to their patrons that they need not rush home to hear Ed Wynn, but that his show would be presented in the movie theater even if it meant interrupting the motion picture program.

Joe Cook, left below, was a fast-talking comedian who left his audience breathless and exhausted. As a monologist, he had few superiors unless it was "Doc" Rockwell, the original "Quack, quack, quack" man of vaudeville and legitimate theater. Using a skull or banana stalk to illustrate his "scientific" lectures, Rockwell would present a devastating stream of patter. Some claim Rockwell was the finest of all modern monologists. Right, Ed Wynn, "The Perfect Fool."

A typical laugh getter in Ed Wynn's letter-answering department was this:

Dear Chief:

I am a woman of forty-five years of age. I weigh 187 pounds and have just rented an apartment which is in a court. There are no window shades in the bathroom and I am afraid of taking a bath because my neighbors can see in. My landlord won't buy shades. What shall I do?

Out of Shape

Ed Wynn's answer would go something like this:

Dear Out of Shape:

If you are really forty-five years of age and if you really weigh 187 pounds, your landlord doesn't have to buy you window shades. You take a bath and your neighbors will buy the shades.

Fire Chief

129

Joe Penner had the whole country repeating his question: "Wanna buy a duck?" Penner was a dim ancestor of George ("I'll be a dirty bird") Gobel.

Then there were George Moran and Charlie Mack, the "Two Black Crows," a comedy team with a line that went something like this:

Moran: I hear your folks are getting rid of all your horses.
Mack: Only the white horses, they eat too much.
Moran: You mean to say the white horses eat more than the others?
Mack: Yes, the white horses eat twice as much as the black horses.
Moran: How do you explain that?
Mack: There's twice as many of them. We have four white horses and two black horses. So we're getting rid of the white horses and we're going to get black ones.

Or perhaps you may recall an exchange something like this:

Moran: What's an alibi?
Mack: An alibi is proving that you was where you was when you wasn't so that you wasn't where you was when you was.

Joe E. Brown was another old trouper with years on the legitimate stage.

Did you ever make a telephone call from one of those stream-lined drugstore phone booths — the kind which are almost form-fitting? [asks Brown].
I got into one once that was so suffocatingly small that I could barely close the door. And I had to close the door before the light would go on.
Then I found that I couldn't get the phone book far enough from my eyes to read it. In order to get some distance I pushed the door open — while still holding the book open in both hands — and the light went out.
I tried to carry the book outside the booth to look at it, but it was chained to the telephone.

130

Joe E. Brown has many unique characterizations. As far as is known he is the only prominent comedian after whom a baseball field has been named. Furthermore, he is the only well-known comedian who was given a trial in the Big Leagues.

Brown was always a comedian of the old clown type, a mugger by trade. His unusually large mouth and comical expression won him laughs when he deserved them for no other reason. "At some time or other every comedian wants to be a tragedian and every tragedian wants to be a comedian," Brown comments. "But comedy has always been my forte . . . I always considered the physical defects I was born with were tragedy enough."

These were some of the stars who made people laugh as the legitimate theater carried on.

The theater of the early part of the twentieth century featured many talented comedians, some of whom had had their start in burlesque, the minstrel show and the early *Ziegfeld Follies*. Both vaudeville and the legitimate theater featured Fanny Brice, Eddie Cantor, Bobby Clark, George M. Cohan, Marie Dressler, W. C. Fields, Frank Tinney, Eddie Foy, De Wolf Hopper, May Irwin, Al Jolson, Bert Lahr, Victor Moore, Fred Stone, Weber and Fields, Ed Wynn, Nat Wills, and many more during this period.

Joe Jackson has been described as "the greatest comedy act on or off a bicycle." A pantomist of rare talent, Jackson won a vast following especially in vaudeville, repeating his same tramp bike-riding act year in and year out. When he died, his son, Joe Jackson, Jr., capably followed in his father's bicycle tracks. Modern television comedians envy this ability to repeat a single comedy act for two generations.

Two teams that made thousands laugh: Ole Olsen and Chic Johnson; Joe Smith and Charles Dale.

The legitimate theater was to provide a range of comedy from *Abie's Irish Rose*, which played over 2,300 consecutive performances in New York, to *Hellzapoppin'*, which held sway at the Winter Garden for a seemingly endless period of time. The effervescent energy of Al Jolson and the perfect foolishness of Ed Wynn provided flesh-and-blood mirth for legitimate theaters.

But even the genius of such comedians was not able in any way to hide the fact that the legitimate theater had received a sledge-hammer blow from the youthful movies. Evidence of this was in the trek of the stars to Hollywood and the fact that vaudeville, born in 1883, finally withered and died in 1932. Some say that it actually never died but merely changed its form. Bob Hope said, "Vaudeville eventually sickened; its trouble was creeping atrophy of the box office muscles induced by the twin viruses, talking movies and radio."

There were some during this early period who refused to recognize the threat to legitimate theater of the motion pictures. Said *Variety* in the early period:

The tendency of the people, especially the middle and lower classes, particularly the children of all classes, to go to the moving pictures has caused some uneasiness, but we are still of the same opinion, after long observation, that was expressed in these columns months ago, viz: that the moving picture cannot supersede vaudeville or burlesque.

Nevertheless, if the silent films seriously threatened the legitimate theater, the coming of talkies sounded the death knell of vaudeville, helped bury burlesque, and created such serious problems for the legitimate theater that it has not to this day been able fully to solve them.

For Laughing Out Loud

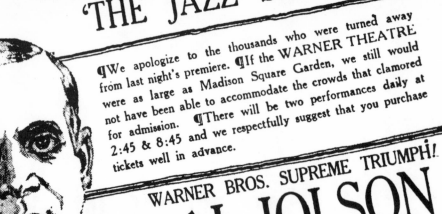

Jolson "Out-Jolsons" Jolson in 'THE JAZZ SINGER'!

¶We apologize to the thousands who were turned away from last night's premiere. ¶If the WARNER THEATRE were as large as Madison Square Garden, we still would not have been able to accommodate the crowds that clamored for admission. ¶There will be two performances daily at 2:45 & 8:45 and we respectfully suggest that you purchase tickets well in advance.

WARNER BROS. SUPREME TRIUMPH!

AL JOLSON in

"THE JAZZ SINGER"

with VITAPHONE

Based upon the play by SAMSON RAPHAELSON as produced on the spoken stage by LEWIS & GORDON and SAM H. HARRIS

A WARNER BROS. PRODUCTION   Directed by ALAN CROSLAND

Cantor Josef Rosenblatt is seen and heard on the VITAPHONE during the concert scene of "THE JAZZ SINGER"

WARNER THEA. B'way at 52d   TWICE DAILY 2:45 — 8:45 SUN. MAT at 3. MATS. 50c, 75c, $1.10, except Sat. & Sun. NIGHTS 75c to $2.20

It's been well known for a long time that talking can get you into a lot of trouble. Any comedian can tell you that. But how much trouble?

Nobody would have guessed.

Not only did talking movies help bury vaudeville, minstrels, burlesque, the circus and much of night clubbing, but they also threw scores of super movie stars out of work. Ever since old Dr. Lee DeForest produced a film in 1923 not only showing a man dropping a load of empty pie trays, but reproducing the noise, sound motion pictures had been on the horizon.

Of course, nobody really believed that talking movies ever would really challenge the silent films. Even William Fox, who certainly knew a lot about the industry, said: "I don't think that there will ever be the much-dreamed-of talking pictures on a large scale. To have conversation would strain the eyesight and the sense of hearing at once, taking away the restfulness one gets from viewing pictures alone." Another moving-picture industrialist predicted that talkies would not last because "Sound will keep moving picture fans awake — they come in to relax and, maybe, catch a nap!"

But one day the nation woke up to discover that talking pictures were not only a reality but that they were an improvement on silent films. The American public welcomed them with open ears.

Don Juan, featuring John Barrymore, was one of the earliest successful talking pictures. Al Jolson singing in *The Jazz Singer* was a sensational step toward popularizing the talking picture. *Lights of New York* became actually the first 100 per cent talkie. Then followed a whole series of shorts, many of a comic nature. The telegraph and telephone wires were kept hot from coast to coast as producers sought to inveigle vaudeville entertainers to go West.

Jolson himself, whose early experiences with silent movies had soured him with the industry, finally had agreed to star in the screen production of *The Jazz Singer,* a highly successful theatrical show on Broadway starring Georgie Jessel, a talented comedian and entertainer.

The Jazz Singer on the screen was not all talkie. As a matter of fact, all the audience could hear was Jolson singing one song and muttering his famous "You ain't heard nothin' yet." But that was enough. The semi-talkie was an immense success. More people saw and heard Jolson in a week than had ever heard of him previously.

Some vaudeville acts were leary of the offers since they suspected — what proved true in the long run — that this was one of the best ways to demolish a perfectly good act. As a result, many of the vaudeville headliners who went West actually did so only after hurriedly creating a brand-new show for Hollywood use, keeping the old one in mothballs for the good old reliable vaudeville billings which were still the steady bread and butter.

As motion pictures found their voice, it was discovered that many actors and actresses were vocally unphotogenic. John Gilbert, one of the great lovers of the silent screen, had a voice that did not reproduce satisfactorily. His days were numbered. So were those of many others: Lon Chaney refused to appear in talkies because he had to change his voice with every make-up.

Among the early talking pictures was *The Coconuts*, featuring four rollicking, hare-brained, disreputable-appearing advocates of slapstick and roughhouse calling themselves the Four Marx Brothers.

The Marx Brothers were actually five in number. They gradually whittled down to four and finally emerged as three. Today a lone member of the group holds forth prominently on television — Groucho.

The Coconuts was a hilarious success. The Marx Brothers, who could not possibly have ventured an effort in the silent films and still been true to their private brand of insanity, proved tremendous on the talking screen. This picture started the brothers on a long career of frantic comedy which did much to alter the course of fun making in the United States.

A verbal description of the Marx Brothers' type of comedy presents difficulties. Perhaps the nearest approach would be to imagine, if you can, painting a mustache on the upper lip of a fierce and mature bull, placing a lit cigar between his lips, teaching him to play the harp and the piano, and to speak English with an Italian accent. Then turn him loose in a china shop. This is the Marx Brothers.

The brothers came to the talkies via Broadway where they had succeeded in destroying scenery, musical instruments, and entire orchestras in musical comedies, to the overwhelming approval of their enthusiastic audiences. They were Harpo, Groucho, Chico, Zeppo and Gummo.

Once the Marx Brothers, all subject to the draft, reported as a group to a Chicago recruiting station to enlist. But they were not successful. One was rejected because of bad eyes, a second had flat feet, a third just recently recovered from an operation and the fourth was rejected for general reasons.

The Three Marx Brothers, Harpo at the harp; Chico at the piano; and Groucho at the horn.

The Marx Brothers produced a series of motion pictures, each one zanier than the other, including: *Coconuts, A Day at the Races, A Night at the Opera, Room Service.*

Just before departing Groucho boasted to the recruiting sergeant: "That's nothing. You should see the fifth Marx Brother: two heads!"

Groucho: Do you know what a blueprint is?
Chico: Sure, oysters.
Groucho: We're going to have an auction.
Chico: I came over here on the Atlantic Auction.
Groucho: We have a quota. Do you know what a quota is?
Chico: Sure, I got a quota (he takes a coin out of his pocket).

Groucho was always master of the zany monologue. Here he is as auctioneer:

Now, folks, we'll take Lot Number 25. Right over there where you're standing. Say, would you mind taking your feet off that lot? You're getting it dirty. Now here's a lot. Oh, I know it doesn't look very big on top, but it goes down as far as you want to go. Now, then, what am I offered for Lot Number 25? What am I offered for Lot Number 25 and a set of O'Henry? What am I offered for O'Henry? Does anybody want to buy a set of dishes? I'll wrestle anybody in the crowd for five bucks.

After a brief interruption, Groucho continues:

Eight hundred residences will be built right here. They are as good as up. Better. You can have any kind of house you want. You can even get stucco. Oh, how you can get stucco. Now is the time to buy while the new boom is on. Remember a new boom sweeps clean. And don't forget the guarantee. If these lots don't double themselves in a year, I don't know what you can do about it.

Jimmy, the well-dressed man. Jimmy Durante was one of the many Broadway entertainers who found Hollywood's talking films a perfect medium for his talents.

139

Talkies were a perfect medium for most comedians. One such was Red Skelton, whose type of wild physical comedy established him as one of the leading of the nation's comedians. Like Groucho and many other successful comedians, Skelton was a master at the ad lib or spontaneous remark. As a friend once said:

Directing Red Skelton is like packing a trunk. You always have twice as much stuff as you have room for. You start with a carefully worked out schedule, a perfectly timed script. On the very next scene, Red comes up with an idea for a bit of business or a line of funny dialogue.

"But we haven't room for it, Red," I protest.

"I won't take but a minute," Skelton says.

It's too good to ignore. We include it in the scene. Then comes the question: What will we drop out to make room for it? "Oh, well," I think, "we'll make that up by dropping something out later."

That never works. The next scene finds Red once more popping up with a new and fancy bit that we add. He is a veritable fountain of comedy lines and business. One gag line reminds him of another and that one of still one more.

Danny Kaye, dancer, singer, master of mimicry and a comedian of ability, has been concentrating in recent years on establishing better international relations. A recent movie made for the United Nations International Children's Emergency Fund (UNICEF) was *Assignment Children*. At right, Danny is shown with a seven-year-old child in Tungkaponghow, a village in Thailand. The picture was distributed globally by Paramount, in nineteen languages.

Among the new comedians whom the talking films brought forward was a thin, wiry, red-haired young man by the name of Danny Kaye, a product of New York night clubs, whose versatility included singing, dancing and comic pantomime comparable to the greatest comedians.

When he was seen playing his now famous *Anatole of Paris* number in a night club, a part for him was immediately written into *Lady in the Dark,* a successful Broadway show. Danny had his salary doubled, tripled, and received a percentage of the gross profits, so successful was he in his first performance. Shortly thereafter he became the first comedian to play the New York Paramount for five consecutive weeks. His entry into the moving pictures was sensational with his *Up in Arms* reaching world-wide success. Danny has shown great interest in the world as his audience and is called "The Uncrowned King of English Entertainment."

Much of Danny's free time is now devoted to the United Nations International Children's Emergency Fund. He recently took a trip around the world for UNICEF equipped with a cameraman. The result was a documentary called, *Assignment Children,* distributed nationally as a public service by Paramount Pictures Corp. with all proceeds going to UNICEF. This was one of Danny Kaye's outstanding moving-picture achievements.

Another innovation in the new talking pictures was the coming of Robert Benchley, former theater critic and vaudeville comedian. Benchley's type of humor is at the opposite pole from that of the Marx Brothers. Being completely without props of any kind unless a starched white shirt and a sheaf of papers are props, his costume is a street suit, his characterization presumably that of himself: a meek, self-conscious, average man-about-town. His early shorts such as his famous *The Treasurer's Report* became classics in the talking film industry:

I shall take but a very few moments of your time this evening, for I realize that you would much rather be listening to this interesting entertainment than to a dry financial statement . . . but I *am* reminded of a story — which you have probably all of you heard.

It seems that there were these two Irishmen walking down the street when they came to a — oh, I should have said in the first place that the parrot which was hanging out in *front* of the store — or rather belonging to one of these two fellows — the *first* Irishman, that is — was — well, *any*way, this parrot —

Now in connection with reading this report, there are one or two points which Dr. Murnie wanted brought up in connection with it, and he has asked me to bring them up in connec — to bring them up.

In the first place, there is the question of the work which we are trying to do up there at

To Hollywood went Broadway's funniest: Judy Holliday; Bert Lahr; Bud Abbott and Lou Costello; Robert Benchley; Joe E. Brown; George Moran and Charlie Mack (Two Black Crows).

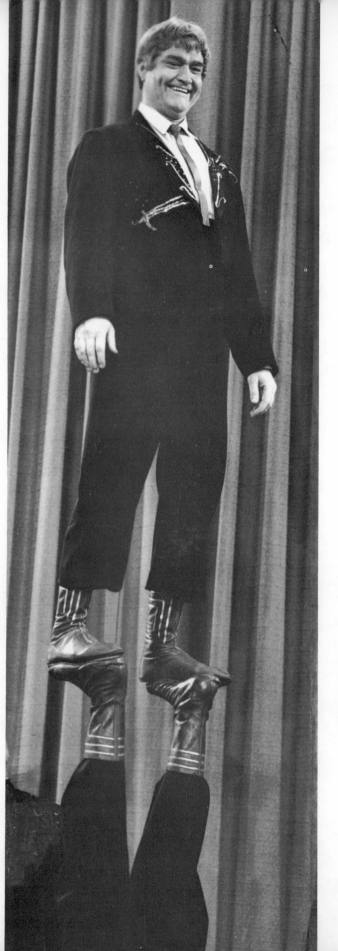

Red Skelton carried on the traditional physical clown comedy which has been a steady laugh provoker since memory began. Here he is shown exhibiting one of his many talents in talkie: *Public Pigeon No. 1.*

our little place at Silver Lake, a work which we feel not only fills a very definite need in the community but also fills a very definite need — er — in the community. I don't think that many members of the Society realize just how big the work is that we are trying to do up there. For instance, I don't think that it is generally known that most of our boys are between the age of fourteen. We feel that, by taking the boy at this age, we can get closer to his real nature — for a boy *has* a very real nature, you may be sure — and bring him into closer touch not only with the school, the parents, and with each other, but also with the town in which they live, the country to whose flag they pay allegiance, and to the — ah — town in which they live.

Now the fourth point which Dr. Murnie wanted brought up was that in connection with the installation of the new furnace last Fall. There seems to have been considerable talk going around about this not having been done quite as economically as it might-have-been-done, when, as a matter of fact, the whole thing *was* done just as economically as possible — in fact, even *more* so. I have here a report of the Furnace Committee, showing just how the whole thing was handled from start to finish.

. . . Now, these figures bring us down only to October. In October my sister was married, and the house was all torn up, and in the general confusion we lost track of the figures for May and August. All those wishing the *approximate* figures for May and August, however, may obtain them from me in the vestry after the dinner, where I will be with pledge cards for those of you who wish to subscribe over and above your annual dues, and I hope that each and every one of you here tonight will look deep into his heart and [archly] into his pocketbook, and see if he can not find it there to help us to put this thing over with a bang [accompanied by a wholly ineffectual gesture representing a bang] and to help and make this just the biggest and best year the Armenians have ever had . . . I thank you.

Once on their way, the talking motion pictures devoured everything within sight. Their charm was irresistible, their influence tremendous. Within three years after

Among the comedians who went into talkies was a song-and-dance man named Bob Hope. Soon the nation was laughing at Hope's jokes and it has been laughing ever since.

The *Three Stooges* hold some sort of record for longevity. Moe Howard, Larry Fine and the late Shemp Howard began the two-reel comedy series in 1933. The team has continued uninterruptedly since then. When one of the trio, Shemp Howard, died in 1957, he was replaced by Joe Besser. The *Three Stooges* have issued some two hundred short comedies and are still going strong.

the first talking motion picture, twenty thousand out of twenty-two thousand motion-picture theaters in the country had rewired for sound. Comedians such as W. C. Fields, Burns and Allen, Fanny Brice, Will Rogers, Eddie Cantor, Al Jolson became stars of the talking films.

Whereas their audiences previously were more or less limited, they now reached millions from one end of the country to the other, wherever a motion-picture theater was located. Not only were the visages of the stars transported nationally and internationally as in the days of the silent films, but their voices, their intonations, their personalities, the very breath they drew, the very sighs they uttered became part of the folklore of the country.

Who would have guessed that the mighty talking motion pictures — that had so greedily rushed to destroy great sections of the legitimate theatrical entertainment world — was itself to be half-devoured by still a new entertainment medium? And casualties in comedians were high in many other fields as well.

146

11

Laugh Makers: by Night and by Day

It's getting so that the job of being a comedian can be ranked with that of the glass blower, the harness maker and the corset fitter.

Professions in which a comedian may operate have been dwindling. The minstrel show and burlesque, favorite minor league for big-time funnymen, are gone.

The circus has folded its tents and many clowns are looking for serious jobs. Vaudeville is a thing of the past and the revue, once so useful as a comedian's paradise, is being counted out.

Night clubs are fewer in number and fearful of their future. The slapstick movie comedy is gone and, for all practical purposes, so is the two-reeler which gave jobs to so many laugh makers.

Many of our entertainment stars in the comic field had their origin in the burlesque or related fields. These include Bobby Clark, Fanny Brice, Bert Lahr, Phil Silvers, Jack Haley, W. C. Fields, Eddie Cantor, Leon Errol, Jimmy Durante, Joe E. Brown, Jack Pearl, and others.

Burlesque, of course, was not always the strip-tease spectacle that it became in its latter years. At the turn of the century, burlesque was a family-type entertainment. Its roots go back to the early days when such great entertainers as George L. Fox made a national reputation burlesquing famous public figures and theatrical characters. But as the competition of the motion pictures developed, burlesque found itself fighting a losing battle.

It struggled to stave off its doom. It resorted more and more to undressed girls in the strip-tease and less and less to the traditional comedian. Many burlesque comedians, as a matter of fact, drifted to Hollywood where they were absorbed as Mack Sennett Keystone cops. Movies absorbed them as the radio and TV were to do in the future.

Many a comedian was to find his early training in burlesque of tremendous value in the coming new entertainment mediums.

Night clubs really obtained their start in the days of Prohibition following World War I. It was a federal crime to buy an alcoholic drink and special clubs or "speakeasies" were established mainly to sell liquor underground. Those were hectic days and the flaunting of the Prohibition Law tended to encourage the establishment of the night club.

The comedian has played an important part in the night club in all of its stages of development.

During Prohibition days one of the most famous of all night-club comedians to come to the fore was Jimmy Durante. "Of all the box-office attractions that got a start in the clubs," Durante is reported to have said, "not one ever stepped in by way of vaudeville or musical comedy, while some of the best stage headliners failed

Yes, that's Jimmy Durante at the piano. He is with a group of youthful night-club entertainers in the early days of his career. "He would be a great comic even with a snub nose," one critic commented.

149

to click in the night clubs. Texas Guinan, Van and Schenck, Harry Richman, and others, built their following in the clubs. It's funny, though. None of them who later took to the stage experienced difficulty in building a theater following. There is a difference in technique between working in the intimate space of a night club and the vastly greater one of the theater."

It was during his night-club days that Jimmy received the name of "Schnozzola." As he describes it, "Jack Duffy, of the vaudeville team of Bernard and Duffy christened me . . . came into the Alamo one night and I asked him to do a number. 'Sure, Schnozzola,' he said, 'What will it be?' Before that I had always been 'Ragtime Jimmy,' now I'll never be anything but Schnozzola."

Jimmy had been merely a night-club piano player up to the time he met Lou Clayton and Eddie Jackson, both dancers and able night-club entertainers. The team of Clayton, Jackson and Durante was to become one of the most successful comedy teams in the history of American entertainment. Occasionally Jimmy would leave his piano to engage in a little singing. Up to that time he had never cracked a joke. As he put it, "Once in a while I would sing a song through one of dem megraphones. But I didn't even do much singin'. I never had much of a verce."

Encouraged by friends, in particular, Sime Silverman, editor of *Variety,* to open up their own night club, the trio decided to call the enterprise the Club Durante, but when the sign was installed, Jimmy noticed that it read "Club Durant." Jimmy protested that an "e" was missing. But the person in charge said that an additional "e" would cost an additional $100. Since money was short the partners decided to let the sign stand as it was; and one of the most famous of all night-club spots went down in history with a misspelled name.

150

The trio, Clayton, Jackson and Durante, were a comedy threesome who "wowed them" in night clubs, vaudeville, and on the legitimate stage. Jimmy is shown at left with Frances Williams, Eddie Jackson and Lou Clayton. Right, Jimmy at the "pianner."

It was not long before the Club Durant became the rage of New York with the team of Clayton, Jackson and Durante engaging in the beginnings of their type of roughhouse, wild-man comedy which was to be the sensation of the night-club after-dark crowd. Upon visiting the Club Durant, George M. Cohan murmured, "Don't those guys ever sit down?"

Damon Runyon stated in print, "I doubt if a greater café combination ever lived." At a later date the well-known critic, Brooks Atkinson, was to describe Jimmy as "burning his way across the stage, splintering the English language, assaulting his companions, hurling hats into the orchestra pit, whirling around to confront an imagined adversary, bursting with undisciplined energy."

While the team of Clayton, Jackson and Durante was a talented one, it became apparent that Jimmy provided the touch of lovable genius which was creating a national entertainment sensation. Durante's nose was on its way — as Gene Fowler put it — to "becoming the most widely known promontory this side of Gibraltar."

Sometimes people would ask Clayton whether it was he who helped Jimmy achieve his high place. "God gave Jimmy Durante his great talent," Clayton answered. "A thousand Lou Claytons never could have put that talent into this man. But I loved him and I knew then as I know now that he was a true genius in his own way. And he was so sweet and fine that I never could get enough of this man."

Other comedians showed an amazing lack of envy toward Durante despite his growing success. Red Skelton had this to say in explanation: "It's because none of us can steal from him. Imitations of Durante fall flat, for he is in a class by himself."

"He would be a great comic even with a snub nose," said Ashton Stevens, the distinguished drama critic.

151

Joe E. Lewis, talented night-club comedian, used to be confused with the fighter Joe Louis. So he picked an initial "E" because Joey is the traditional name of the clown. Joe E. Lewis is more than a clown. He is rated as the funniest sophisticated entertainer in America.

Bert Lahr, right, had his start in burlesque and vaudeville. His shows included *Delmar's Revels*, *Hold Everything* and *DuBarry was a Lady*.

Dean Martin and Jerry Lewis were a successful laugh combination before they went their own separate ways. When they were on stage together, anything could happen.

The fact is that Jimmy Durante, through his night-club entertainment, brought something new to the American comedy scene. He, together with Clayton and Jackson, introduced a form of whirlwind comedy, physical in its major aspects with its hat-throwing, piano-breaking, mad-clown antics. But there was something more to it than rough-and-tumble shenanigans which characterized the Clayton, Jackson and Durante bill of fare. The spark which ignited the team was Jimmy himself and his spontaneous type of humor which seemed to flow from him as naturally as mutterings from a W. C. Fields or a Mammy song from an Al Jolson.

When Jimmy left night-clubbing he had some doubt that he could succeed in a medium which was less intimate than the night club. He need not have worried. The Durante personality was to sweep the nation in whatever medium he turned to, vaudeville, musical comedy, motion pictures, radio or television. Night-clubbing never fully recovered from his loss.

Another great comedian in the arena of after-dark entertainment is Joe E. Lewis, frequently described as "the Funniest Man in the World," or "King of the Night Clubs."

Jimmy Savo, veteran of revues, musical comedies and night clubs, was originally a child-wonder juggler. He starred as rope-walker, dancer, singer, comedian, pantomimist.

Lewis originally set out as the fastest-talking comedian in Chicago. When he decided to change his night-club job he ran into the middle of a gangster feud which resulted in a brutal attack upon him by three strong-arm assailants. Newspaper headlines carried the story.

CABARET STAR'S THROAT SLASHED! VICIOUS KNIFING SILENCES COMEDIAN! JOE LEWIS STABBED, NEAR DEATH!

All the more tragic was the fact that in the attack, Joe's vocal chords had been severed in addition to other very critical injuries. It was years before the comedian was able to get about. But he courageously insisted upon his intention to return to the entertainment field.

Joe E. Lewis insisted and persisted. In a few years, the comedian rose from a hospital bed to become a night-club entertainer whom the critics would pronounce "a genius" and "one of the greatest."

On April 1, 1953, friends of Joe bought twenty-five pages in *Variety* at $400 a page to commemorate his thirteenth year in show business. The Friars Club page saluted him as "the nicest guy in the world."

154

Regarding Joe Lewis' comedy technique, George Burns of the famed Burns and Allen team says, "Joe E. is an absolute master at comedy gag timing. He's got that certain sense of being able to twist a risqué story, by perfect timing, into a terrifically funny, harmless comedy line." George Jessel in his book *So Help Me* says, "Joe E. is the only comedian with originality to come up within the last ten years." Joe's humor lies largely in his gags.

"You'll notice that I'm doing a very fast show. I'm cutting out all the laughs," he'll say. Or: "These jokes may not sound like much to you but your laughs don't sound like much to me either." Or: "Everybody's breeding things. I crossed a rooster with a rooster — and got a very cross rooster."

Felix Adler is a great modern white-face clown. Some of the most famous former residents of "Clown Alley" have been Fred Stone, Red Skelton, Bobby Clark, Paul McCullough, Joe E. Brown.

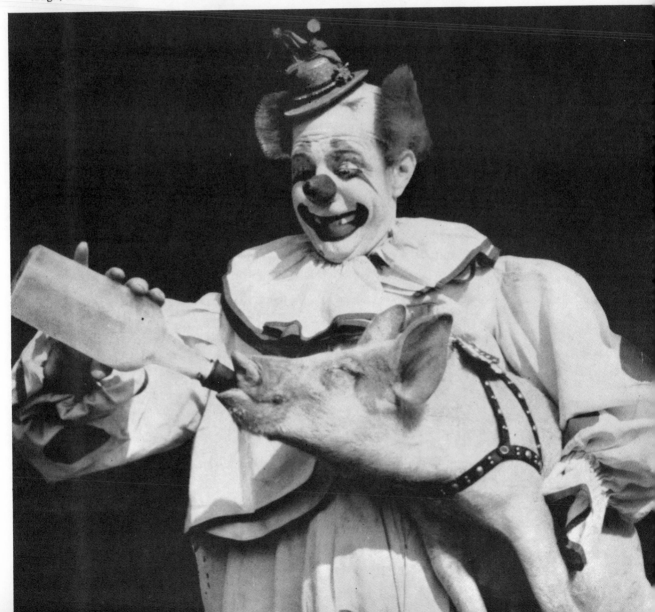

Emmett Kelly, with broom instead of baseball bat, is providing comedy relief in the Big Leagues. One of the greatest circus clowns, Kelly was hired to provide comic entertainment for *Brooklyn Dodger* fans.

Abel Green, the astute editor of *Variety,* describes the Lewis type of humor as follows:

Joe E. Lewis is a show business phenomenon whose work, almost literally, is his play and vice versa, because he's doing what comes naturally. Almost a gypsy in reality . . . he is at home in all the gayer cities of America, and could virtually call seventy-five per cent of them his home. His homes away from home are what dissipate the legend about the necessity to call something, some place, his home.

Underneath his avowed vagabondia is a realistic awareness that the business of being a fool brooks no foolishness. The mobs and the snobs, the effete set and the mugs, the borscht belt and the Texas oil tycoons, all dig his stuff. By gearing his material to the heps he also knows how to perform for the squares or, at least, the so-called not-so-initiate. That's where his pixie personality proves potent because, in even more rarefied atmosphere, he has gotten away with some slick nifties which, under other auspices, would be pedestrian. What is one man's B. S. Pully comes out ultra-sly divertissement with which only a Lewis seemingly can get away.

His capacity for friendship is as much a part of his basic box-office appeal as his talent. There is no minimizing his wide personal following, some of it almost bordering on a cult. Result is that Lewis can do no wrong, be it with the press or pundits. In certain key cities as much as ninety per cent of his draw is personal, or customers who feel that they have an almost personal relationship with him. It is said that Lewis, by phone, could raise a couple of million if he wanted to go into the racetrack, bistro or any other business.

Of course, there were many other talented stars who passed through the night-club arena. Dean Martin and Jerry Lewis, Joey Adams, Jerry Lester, Henny Youngman, Sophie Tucker, Jimmy Savo, Danny Thomas and many others.

During the same period when many comedians were going into the night clubs, a new brand of comedian emerged into the bright sunlight — the baseball clown. There haven't been many of them but they have represented a significant form of comedy.

Al Schacht and Nick Altrock were two baseball clowns who entertained millions of people in their day.

Comedy and sports are traditional in America and you might say that the great

Al Schacht, "clown prince of baseball," brought clowning and pantomime to the baseball field in a professional way. Schacht has played personally before more people than any entertainer in the history of the country.

157

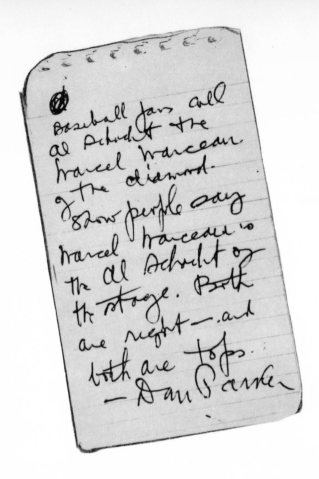

American pastime is either telling jokes or playing ball. Or to put it another way, many of our most popular Americans have either been comedians or ballplayers.

When Joe E. Brown, who happens to represent a combination of baseball player and comedian, was taking part in a workout with the New York Yankees one day in his early years, Miller Huggins, manager of the team, studied Brown's playing form intently for a few moments before he said, "Well, he's not the first comedian I've seen in a Yankee uniform."

The comedy of a Ring Lardner also flows from our great national pastime, baseball. Al Schacht is not only an outstanding baseball comedian but also a professional ballplayer in his own right as well as the author of several books.

Schacht's humor was largely pantomime representing take-offs of baseball stars, tennis players, boxers, and almost anyone who lent himself to physical satire. "Before the coming of television," Schacht says, "I entertained more people than any entertainer in the country. When I put on a show at the Yankee Stadium more people would watch me than would see Al Jolson in an entire season. When you're on the baseball field you can't explain your comedy. You have to act it."

But while the legitimate stage and the world of entertainment in general (by night and by day) was carrying on, a gigantic firecracker was lit and spluttering, ready to go off with a boom.

158

12

Funny Air

There was something wonderful about radio in the early days. A performer need not be beautiful. Nor dress well. You could even let down your suspenders and loosen your girdle while you were on the air.

Radio was the great equalizer. No matter how you looked, how much money you owned, how you dressed, it was only your voice that reached the people outside.

For example, there is the anecdote concerning Al Jolson and his protégé at the time, Harry Richman. Although Jolson himself refused to go on the air, Richman was persuaded to do so and sang his ballads regularly for a period of a year or so.

When Jolson finally turned his talents to the radio, the audience did not know who he was but thought they detected a familiar quality in his way of singing. "Who is this guy stealing Richman's style?" people asked.

Indeed, how were they to know that Jolson had groomed Richman, taught him much of what he knew?

Soon radio-listening America came to know the real Jolson and laugh at his jokes just as it began to know it was seven o'clock because Amos 'n Andy were on the air. Similarly, all America stayed glued to the radio to hear Jack Pearl, veteran of stage

Fred Allen and his "Allen's Alley" was a weekly Sunday-night radio favorite. At the right, Fred Allen. Left, Mrs. Nussbaum played by Minerva Pious; Titus Moody played by Parker Fennelly; and Senator Claghorn played by Kenny Delmar.

and vaudeville, recreate Baron Munchausen. Could anything be funnier than to hear the Baron ask "Voss you dere, Sharlie?" Obviously that was just about as comical as it was possible to get at the time.

Of course, there still were those who thought radio was an interesting gadget but just couldn't see it as a commercial enterprise. For example, a widely respected advertising publication stated:

> Any attempt to make the radio an advertising medium, in the accepted sense of the term, would, we think, prove positively offensive to great numbers of people. The family circle is not a public place, and advertising has no business intruding there unless it is invited. . . . The man who does not want to read a paint ad in the newspaper can turn the page and read something else. But the man at the end of the radio must listen, or shut it off entirely. That is a big distinction that ought not to be overlooked.

And, of course, in the early days there were the same warnings from the die-hards that had been sounded with the coming of the talking motion pictures. Listening to radio was supposed to be bad for the ears. To have a radio in the house, it was said, was a certain invitation to the starting of fires. But the numbers of radios being sold despite their huge, ugly, bird-nest type of aerials and their myriad of expensive and mysterious tubes continued to go up and up and up; and so did the ratings of some of the new radio stars who were to be heard weekly.

From the start it seems that radio comedians were favorites with the rapidly growing listening audience. Among the top scorers in popularity polls were to be found Eddie Cantor, Fibber McGee and Molly, Ed Wynn, Jack Benny, Fred Allen, Edgar Bergen and Charlie McCarthy, Red Skelton, Amos 'n' Andy, Bob Hope, Al Jolson.

Perhaps the most celebrated of radio's long list of outstanding funnymen was one who had the unique accomplishment of winning respect both from his fellow comedians and the general public — Fred Allen.

Fred Allen was deft with hats as well as words. Like W. C. Fields, he started as a juggler. Later he became one of the most capable ad-lib comedians in the business.

Jack Benny has established a national reputation as a penny-pincher, an egotist and a man whose age seldom advances. He drives an ancient Maxwell pictured at right, and is the rare comedian who is willing to make himself the butt of all the jokes.

162

Allen, a former juggler from Boston, had a dry wit and a ready tongue and the ability to make up funny lines when he happened to have nothing written in his hand at the time. Commenting on the new medium of radio, Mr. Allen said: "Radio has the advantage over the theater. The show doesn't close if there's nobody in the balcony."

According to Steve Allen, also a successful comedian but not — contrary to rumor — Fred Allen's son, Fred was the "King of Radio Comedy." He was "the most quoted comedian of our time."

Jack Benny, center, with band-leader Phil Harris and Eddie Anderson, the "Rochester" of radio and television fame.

Quips from Fred Allen delighted the nation almost as much as those from the tongue or pen of Will Rogers a few years before. Both men, incidentally, were natural descendants from the same stock — Jonathan of the early days of the American Yankee comedy.

"California," quipped Allen, "is a great place to live if you're an orange." Concerning company executives with whom he seemed to have a constant though good-natured feud, Allen once said, "A vice president is a bit of executive fungus that falls on a desk that has been exposed to conference."

Because of his ad-libbing proclivities, Allen frequently found himself in warm or hot water with the authorities. But censoring Allen wasn't always easy. He had a fast tongue and as an ad libber he knew his business. Once when a well-known sponsor was paying him a large salary, he made some biting reference to Scottish thrift and several hundred Scotsmen from the Pittsburg area signed an indignant letter saying that they did not intend ever again to use the product which the sponsor sold.

Since the product happened to be a laxative, Allen had no choice but to make his now-famous apology. "The prospect that they (the protesters) will go through life constipated so frightened the agency that they made me apologize."

Allen was very fearful that the radio released such a huge number of machine-made jokes per night that it dulled the average person's responses. "Before radio," he said, "when a Will Rogers or a Peter Finley Dunne made a wisecrack, it would be quoted from one end of the country to the other and everyone repeated it for a month. Today, nobody remembers what I said on the radio last week, except some gag writers who are figuring ways to steal the jokes."

One of the most amusing of Fred Allen's radio programs was his famous *Allen's Alley* in which he would go from door to door weekly, interviewing three or four carefully developed personalities. Included were Mrs. Nussbaum, played by Minerva Pious; Senator Claghorn, the noisy politician from the deep South, played by Kenny Delmar; Titus Moody, the New England farmer played by Parker Fennelly; and the Irishman Ajax Cassidy played by Peter Donald.

While Fred Allen radiated a satirical sharp self-confidence, his friendly archrival, Jack Benny, was the personification of something quite different. As a matter of fact, Benny has made a living both on radio and television perfecting the fine art of self-humiliation. Someone has said that Jack Benny will outlast all the other comedians because he has one tremendous advantage: he doesn't have to do anything. There is some belief that Benny has brought more laughs to more people than any other entertainer who ever lived. His type of performance involves perfect timing as one of his major accomplishments.

Through the years he has built up an entire characterization of Jack Benny as a

Jack Pearl, dialect comedian, as Baron Munchausen, was one of the big hits of early radio.

stingy, vainglorious, gulled and tyrannized individual who pinches his pennies, whose bark is always more dangerous than his bite, and whose age is always a source of painful sensitivity to him.

His technique, which has lasted him through his many years in the entertainment world, is never to punch too hard so that, should some of his lines fall by the wayside without laughter, the audience seldom knows the difference.

Jack Benny was one of the first performers on the radio to have laughs turned on himself, the star of the program. He developed the character of the man with human frailties. As a matter of fact, he made a career out of developing these human frailties and making them known to millions of people all over the country.

Explaining the humor of his program, Benny once said, "I'm a big shot, see? I'm fast-talking. I'm a smart guy. I'm boasting about how marvelous I am. I am a marvelous lover. I'm a marvelous fiddle player. Then five minutes after I start shooting

Charles Correll and Freeman Gosden (left) originally went on the air in a *Sam 'n' Henry* skit. In 1928, they began their *Amos 'n' Andy* program and soon became a national comedy institution. Below is Ed Wynn as the *Fire Chief*. Wynn was the first radio star to insist that a live audience be present for his broadcasts.

Left, the beloved husband-and-wife team of Fibber McGee and Molly played on the radio for many years by Marian and Jim Jordan.

Right, Edgar Bergen and his wooden-headed partner Charlie McCarthy, a ventriloquist act that had all radio-listening America laughing. When Charlie was made mascot of the Chicago White Sox, he remarked "some of my relatives are bats."

There have been many comedy teams in the entertainment world but none more successful in radio than George Burns and Gracie Allen.

off my mouth, my cast makes a schmo out of me. Wherever I go, whatever I do, I
get into trouble for no good reason at all."

Many of the outstanding comedians of today confess the debt they owe to Benny.
Fred Allen once said, "Practically all comedy shows on the radio today owe their
structure to Benny's conceptions. He was the first to realize that the listeners are not
in a theater with a thousand other people, but are in a small circle at home. The
Benny show is like a one-man's family in slapstick. When they tune in to the Benny
show, it's like tuning in to somebody else's home.

"Benny also was the first comedian in radio to realize that you could get big laughs
by ridiculing yourself instead of your stooges. Benny became a fall guy for everybody
else on his show."

Getrude Berg as Mollie in "The Goldbergs" has a unique position of love in the hearts of radio and television audiences.

Never pushing, never aggressive, the Benny style goes something like this:

Here it is seven days until Christmas and I hate to admit it, but I haven't even begun to do my Christmas shopping. I guess because it's always such a problem for me. There are so many people I have to remember, close associates, Don Wilson, Dennis Day . . . and then there's Rochester. Now, Rochester has been working for me for eighteen years and it's so hard to know what to get him . . . he's got nothing. And Don Wilson . . . there at least I got some help. His wife told me he would like a shirt. She told me his size, 16-33. Now where are you going to find a shirt with a 33 neck and a 16 sleeve? . . . Then there are the boys in my orchestra. Of course, I always exchange gifts with them. And they've already given me mine. They sent me a beautiful five-carat diamond ring. Now there was no card in the gift or anything, but I knew it was from the boys in the orchestra when the police came and took it back. Fortunately, in our next musical arrangement the clarinet player has a ten-year rest. Anyway, the ring does count as a gift so I have to reciprocate. Now on Christmas I usually give Frankie Remley, my guitar player, a bottle of bourbon. But this year his doctor absolutely refuses to let him have any liquor . . . so I got Remley something else. He was just thrilled. I gave him the name of a new doctor . . .

Bob Hope, one of the talented young comedians who became a national figure as a result of radio, bases a large part of his comedy approach on his careful timing, just as does Jack Benny. And, like Benny, Hope also uses self-ridicule as a means of getting laughs. If every joke he made about the size of his nose paid off in money, he could afford to have his nose fixed many times over.

One of the first things that Hope learned in the entertainment field was patience: "One of the things I learned was to have enough courage to wait," Hope states. "I'd stand there waiting for them to get it [the joke] for a long time, longer than any other comedian had enough guts to wait. My idea was to let them know who was running things."

Thus Hope will crack a joke whether on the stage, on radio or television and bravely wait it out until the very interlude of waiting has become almost a national symbol for hilarity when Hope is the comedian involved.

Hope has a reputation in some circles for being a mere repeater of gag chatter written by his ghosts. Whether this is true or not, he has perfected his manner of presenting lines until today he has become an institution. A sample of his radio comedy monologue indicates the general type of humor which has made Hope famous:

I'm a little tired tonight. I'm building a new house in North Hollywood and I want to

At right Colonel Lemuel Q. Stoopnagle and Bud Hulich, a popular radio team.

tell you that's hard work. I think I'll have to hire a carpenter to help me. It's one of those California all-weather houses . . . you know, six rooms, a big sun porch . . . and a direct wire to the coastguard! I decided to build a permanent home now that I'm doing pretty well in pictures. Of course, it's the only house on the block with wheels on it, but I'm really putting up a nice house. The other day when the lumber came in . . . the termites were standing around smacking their lips and applauding. You'll like the inside of the house. It's really got a beautiful bathroom . . . when you want cold water, all you have to do is dig . . . when you want hot water, you just go deeper! It's got three guest rooms . . . the green room, the blue room, and the jade room. It's really all the same room . . . we just change the lights for the first two and burn incense for the other! And I've got a new idea in the bedroom . . . the walls just pull out from a bed. I have a Murphy bed and a Morris chair in my room, the room is so small. The other morning Murphy woke up with an accent!

While this type of humor may not seem complex, the art of being a stand-up

Bob and Ray, two men of madness and mirth, are really Bob Elliot and Ray Goulding. They started as disc jockeys and developed a fresh brand of humor on radio and, later, TV.

Two successful radio combinations: the Ritz Brothers (Al, Jimmy and Harry) (above) and Garry Moore and Jimmy Durante (right).

comedian is not an easy one. Hope developed it from dance routine into a gag man. Part of his success is his ability to study his audience and to angle his jokes to fit the mood or background or current events of a given situation.

Another pioneer of the early radio days was Ed Wynn (The Perfect Fool) who had achieved an enviable reputation as a comedian in burlesque and on the musical comedy stage. When he took to radio, Wynn achieved even greater popularity as the famous "Fire Chief." Wynn was the first of the great comedians to broadcast from a stage with an actual admission-paying audience. The practice became standard after a time and has been the source of helping many comedians establish rapport with their audiences, something badly needed for laugh making. Commenting upon the contrast between his legitimate stage activity and the radio, Ed Wynn said ruefully, "I spent $750,000 publicizing myself as the Perfect Fool. And almost overnight it is forgotten and I am known only as the Fire Chief."

His good friend Fred Allen described how Ed Wynn obtained his first radio job: "When Wynn was being considered for radio," said Allen, "he was starring on Broadway in his own show, *The Laugh Parade*. To make sure that Ed, who had been a star in the theater practically all of his life, would be suitable for the radio program, a group of officials decided to attend Ed's show. To double check on how Ed would come over the air, the executives sat through Ed's entire show with their eyes closed. P.S.: When they opened their eyes, Ed got the job."

Although Jimmy Durante had been a star in night club and legitimate stage, with the coming of radio he teamed up with young Garry Moore to become a sensational success on the new medium. Garry's ability to ad lib was a great asset in his teaming up with Durante since Jimmy himself was unpredictable and needed a fast-stepping partner to keep up with him.

It was on the radio that Jimmy made nationally popular some of his famous songs. It was on the radio that his "Goodnight, Mrs. Calabash, wherever you are" first became familiar to millions of people.

Many stars brightened the early radio days and actually became national institutions for many years. Fibber McGee and Molly became family favorites as did the Goldbergs, featuring Gertrude Berg. There were, of course, Amos 'n' Andy, the Happiness Boys, Burns and Allen, Stoopnagle and Budd, Eddie Cantor, and Henry Morgan.

Even Will Rogers took to the air and it was his impersonation of President Calvin Coolidge which caused such confusion nationally. Rogers had designed his imitation to be an obvious joke but so many people were deceived by it that he was forced to apologize for the impersonation.

Household radio grew to such an extent that almost everyone had a set and most people unconsciously blessed the fact that they could listen to music or to a comedian and at the same time use their eyes for other things — cooking, homework, reading, writing letters. . . .

But the reign of the Ear was not to last forever. The almighty Eye was to have its day — and soon. . . .

174

13

Now You See It

"Television is nothing like vaudeville," Fred Allen once commented. "In vaudeville you had one act and a constantly changing audience—TV, like radio, is just the opposite. You have the same audience all the time, so the act must be changed after each performance. Naturally, the quality of the material gets low."

Jim Bishop, biographer of the comedian, Jackie Gleason, wrote:

> Television is the most perpetually baffling invention since the one-way street.
>
> It is, in one breath, the savior of actors and their executioners. It creates and it kills.
>
> A man may work for months or years to draw up a good animal act. In the days of vaudeville he could tour the country for two years or more, at $125 a week, without ever meeting the same audience twice.
>
> Today he puts his act on a television network show and, in six minutes, he has been seen by fifty million persons, has earned $500, and his act is finished. It cannot be shown again. Theatrically, he is dead.

Comedians were not slow in expressing themselves regarding their greatest boon and bug-a-boo.

"When the lumber barons went through a forest," Sid Caesar said, "they took everything they wanted and didn't bother to reseed or to heal the leftover trees that were hurt by exposure to the elements. Then came a law correcting this. TV has no such law. It should. The networks have gone through the forests of comedians, and they have done nothing to replace them or to help the old stars fight exposure."

Bert Lahr developed his comedy talent from the early burlesque, vaudeville and musical comedy. "There is no place today for comedians to develop," he said. "There is no burlesque, no vaudeville. Just a few clubs and television."

Groucho Marx defended the comedian. "A lot of network and advertising men can't make up their own minds whether a TV show is good or not."

Ed Wynn believed that it was dangerous to have the network and advertising experts sit in judgment on the comedian. "Being a comedian is an art and not a business. It should not be judged exclusively by business standards."

"TV has helped and injured the development of comedy," Steve Allen commented. "It has helped it by stimulating it to a prodigious growth, but the very speed of that growth in the long run seems to have worked to the disadvantage of the art of comedy. The industry seems to wear many of the comics out and to cut off the progress of newcomers before they have a fair chance to develop."

Milton Berle, the first casualty of television, began his career by playing in some fifty films without a comedy line in any of them. He rose through vaudeville, musical comedy and *Ziegfeld Follies* and was the first big-name comedian to appear on TV. In 1948 he became known as "Mr. Television." "His programs," commented the *New Yorker*, "are said to have so powerful a hold on the TV public that shopkeepers who would ordinarily be open for business between 8 and 9 on Tuesday evenings now close down their stores for lack of customers."

Lou Holtz, a popular comedian of the 1930's, said: "You can't stay successful every week as a comedian . . . Al Jolson was the greatest . . . but remember this. The people out of town saw him, at the most, about three times a year. When he arrived in Minneapolis or Seattle or anyplace else it was a big event. I'm pretty sure if Jolson sang and clowned for them on television every Wednesday night, by the time he went into his second or third year, they'd be turning him off."

Red Buttons was a promising young comedian when he entered TV. "Red had definite talent," said one TV executive. "It seems he just ran out of gas. He was good for one big season, but he had a limited amount of tricks to last in this business . . ."

Sam Levenson, another comedian with a serious approach, pointed out: "Great jokes don't grow on trees. Great jokes have to ripen. TV burns up subject matter faster than it can often be produced."

Mack Sennett, dean of modern laugh makers, asked: "What's happened to laughter? There used to be so much of it!"

Harold Lloyd asked whether the weekly pace was to blame. "We used to produce a two-reel silent comedy every week, month after month," Lloyd recalled. "And they were funny and did not seem to run out of material. True, we often used to scratch our heads and wonder what we would use for gags. But we managed somehow. And the public didn't seem to tire of them . . . We never knew from day to day or hour to hour what we would do to bring the laughs. Most of our humor was spontaneous and without written scripts."

The influential magazine *Advertising Age* joined the discussion:

The merciless march of television program is about to wipe out almost all comedians . . . . The saddest part of this story is that there are no training grounds left for young comics. Gone is the classic burlesque, the Chautauqua circuit, vaudeville, radio, movies, revue in the legitimate theatre, or any of the try-out places. Television has, ironically enough, wiped out these old starting gates.
Above all America wants to laugh. After a day of competing, the old man wants to come home to a good laugh. The world needs funny men. . . . Somebody has to take a chance on the new comics or on the old ones who are coming back. . . .

Variety was keenly concerned with the growing crisis facing today's comedians:

Television comedians with weekly exposure are disappearing at an unprecedented clip . . . . Moreover, there won't be anybody around to replace the departing comedians. . . . Like the warnings about the impossibility of the task of furnishing comics with enough material to perform on a week-in week-out basis, the warnings that television must develop fresh young talent have come true. . . .

In an article "Clowns in Decline," *The New York Times* observed in 1957, "After thirty years of unchallenged dominance it now seems generally conceded that comedians no longer are the mainstay of broadcasting. The inexorable law of overexposure has caught up with the majority of clowns. Today, as a class, they are not as important as Western dramas."

The history of comedy shows that the great comedians, while often using the same routine, entered creatively into every performance. Whether it was Joseph Jefferson in *Rip Van Winkle,* a Weber and Fields revue, or the Marx Brothers in the *Coconuts,* the performance was never exactly the same. Audiences would return again and again to see the same show. A creative process was at work which made each performance different no matter how often seen.

On TV the "ad lib" was—in a period of teleprompters, memorized scripts, ghost writers and vast audiences—considered a foolhardy risk. Even those who could ad lib and who were fast on their mental feet often rehearsed their ad libs to make certain that they did not say something which might offend not just a theater full of people, but the entire nation.

When *Cinderella* was produced on TV in 1957, it was watched—CBS stated in *Variety*—by "an audience of more than 100,000,000—the largest number up to that time to view an entertainment program—enough, as someone pointed out, to fill a Broadway theater seven days a week for 165 years."

Small wonder that the genuine ad lib became so rare as to be almost nonexistent!

"I just take what I see and exaggerate it a little bit," said Sid Caesar. "I pick out the obvious things that everybody is familiar with but never stops to think about."

And yet there were those who wondered why comedy was losing its hold on the people when the very heart of comedy was spontaneity and creativity.

Florenz Ziegfeld would never willingly miss a performance of his star comedian, Will Rogers, because no two performances of Rogers' were ever alike. Rogers avoided rehearsals. Even his fellow performers would gather to hear what he had to say when he was on stage.

Rogers not only insisted on a more or less spontaneous type of delivery; he also based his material on current events, on developing news which could not be exhausted.

Similarly, Weber and Fields built the core of their comedy on satire and parody. While slapstick and gags were the outer surface of the Weber and Fields success, more profoundly, their humor was based on keen scrutiny and reaction to life about them. The same may be said for Harrigan and Hart, F. H. Chanfrau, and many other comedy giants of the past.

In the late 1950's, the use of parody, satire and critical comment as source material for our comedy was almost as rare as the genuine ad lib. Can it be, it was asked, that comedy has passed by spontaneity and newsworthiness as important laugh-producing necessities? If so, it was at odds with the entire history of successful comedy since our nation's beginning.

The New York Times remarked in 1957 on this situation that, "this is evidently no time for comedy, unless it is an amiable jest about family foibles or a report on the war between the sexes. Things used to be different. Authors could poke virile fun at politics, business and babbitry in all its aspects. . . ."

But whatever the reason for the decline of American comedians or comedy, history gave confidence that the decline would be short-lived. Comedy is a persistent commodity. Discouraged or suppressed in one medium, it springs up again in another . . . at a later date.

Few people would have been certain that the 1960's were to witness a rebirth of the comic spirit. And fewer still could have guessed the exact forms the new laugh makers were to assume.

14

Cowboys Instead of Comedians

"We'll laugh them off the air."
"We'll kid the pants off them."

These were the brave words of comedians, quoted by *Variety* in August, 1957, in response to the challenge of the Westerns.

As comedians disappeared from TV screens in homes all over America, badge-wearing sheriffs and gun-toting outlaws galloped on.

TV programs, featuring violence and crime, increased. Gagsters were displaced by gangsters and, for change of pace, there was professional wrestling and sex.

Of course, television was not the only communications medium with a paralyzed funny bone. Radio went the way of its kid brother, TV; only more so. Movies, for the most part, forgot how to be funny. Broadway, deprived for years of burlesque and vaudeville as testing grounds for comedians, turned more and more to sordid themes.

Generally the movement of comedians in the late 1950's was away from TV and toward Broadway. They included Lucille Ball, Wally Cox, George Gobel, Phil Silvers, Art Carney, Sid Caesar and Milton Berle. Only occasionally (except for reruns) did they return to TV during this melancholy era.

"I've done a lot of TV work this year," quipped Berle in a night club appearance. "I fixed two sets yesterday."

Danny Kaye, Bob Hope and Victor Borge used TV appearances sparingly, allowing themselves to appear in specials only occasionally.

Borge, a comedian of top rank, was particularly careful not to outlive his TV welcome, appearing only once or twice a year. Some people, he stated, "always insist on something new. They force the humorist to overexpose himself. . . . If what the performer possesses is valuable, it shouldn't be changed for change's sake. Let him repeat his best stuff. Let new generations see it."

More and more professional comedians turned to serious acting, with various degrees of success. Jackie Gleason, described as "the most celebrated buffoon ever to rise through United States television," did so well as a serious motion-picture actor that it won him a *Time* cover portrait.

Panel shows gave a few comedians, such as Groucho Marx and Henry Morgan, a chance to be funny. But here the comedian tended to be more the stand-up (or sit-down) comedian than the traditional laugh maker.

The talented mimic and comic character actor, Sid Caesar, confided to friends: "I think I'm at the end of the line, I've had it." He told the columnist, Erskine Johnson: "The lawyers and the accountants were starting to take television away from the creators. They wanted me to go on film and they talked about residuals and spin-offs, and reruns and capital gains, and how you can sell the reruns and the spin-offs. They wanted shows with shock treatment, not truth."

Retiring from the leadership of *The New Yorker* magazine, Stephen B. Botsford pointed out that "the thing that's hardest to come by . . . these days is humor." Jerome

Art Carney and Jackie Gleason, from a scene in *The Honeymooners,* for many years one of television's most popular "situation comedies."

183

Two great comedians, Ed Wynn and Dick Van Dyke, although from different eras, made use of physical comedy for laugh making.

Beatty, Jr. wrote in the *Saturday Review* that, "We seem to be so insecure that we can't bear to be laughed at, or to laugh at ourselves, even though . . . we never needed it more."

Some comedians found the going easier in TV's so-called "situation comedies." Here, mom, pop and the kids (or some variation of them) were often the central figures. Professional comedians often become mere actors and actresses speaking lines written by gag writers.

The modern TV situation comedy received its first big push in the 1950s with Lucille Ball's *I Love Lucy* series. Lucille was described by her teammate of yesteryear, Desi Arnaz, as "the world's greatest comedienne." Millions of American TV viewers tended to agree.

Other classic situation comedies of the era included the notable Phil Silvers as *Sergeant Bilko,* Red Skelton's *Freddie, the Free-Loader* and *The Dick Van Dyke Show.*

The situation comedy made it easier for the comedian to survive on TV than any other regularly scheduled form. "Everybody doesn't have to knock himself out," commented Joey Bishop, one of the comedians who made good in a situation routine.

In situation comedies, many talented comedians found themselves unable to fully practice their art; but it was a living. Too often, as *Show* magazine put it, producers "found their formula, and comedy lies dead at their feet."

"No wonder," commented one newspaper, "the kids react to grown-ups as they do. Situation comedy adults are not just square; they are stupid."

"Perhaps," said David Susskind, TV producer whose program, *Open End,* featured a series of important interviews with comedians, "the days of the old knock-about great clown may be over . . . there is no training ground left for him."

Among the few hardy perennials who survived in "traditional" comedy was Red Skelton, called "television's greatest clown."

"In TV's brief history," wrote Marie Torre, TV critic for the *New York Herald-Tribune,* "while the acetylene torch called overexposure has singed and seared one comedian after another, Skelton's popularity has never really stopped growing."

There was at first some question as to whether a physical comedian like Skelton, depending so much on his body movement and acrobatics, could succeed on TV. Perhaps Skelton's success developed from the fact that he was a happy clown in a tragic era. Perhaps, too, the public welcomed the apparent return of the spontaneous "ad lib," even if it was written in the script in advance.

Jack Benny was another durable comedian who appeared to defy the trend. One young comic, marveling at Benny's longevity, commented: "He can get people laughing just by standing there and looking at someone."

Comedians like Skelton and Benny established such a bond of understanding between themselves and their audiences—a sort of lovers' pact—that they seemed able to defy the high mortality rate of TV exposure. "The amazing Benny . . ." reported Gerold Frank in *McCall's* magazine, "has been seen and heard, it could be argued, by more people than any other individual in the history of the world . . . There is nothing spectacular about him—no astonishing habits, no gargantuan whims, no temperamental outbursts . . . His producer calls him 'the healthiest of all comedians.' "

Dick Van Dyke

Lucille Ball won national television acclaim in both her *I Love Lucy* and *The Lucy Show* series. She began her dramatic work at the age of fifteen, appearing on Broadway and then Hollywood where she first served as a chorus girl.

Red Skelton shown as Clem Kadiddlehopper with Carol Lawrence. Red's practice of laughing at his own jokes for most comedians is a dangerous practice.

But laugh makers such as Red Skelton and Jack Benny were the exceptions. Comedy was at a low point in number of practitioners and outlets for expression. It was not, however, to be a permanent condition.

New comedians were in the wings waiting to take the stage. As the 1960s progressed, *Variety* commented: "last major trend in TV were the Westerns. They're now virtually kaput . . . Obviously such a trend—if trend it is—will invite a whole fresh batch of comedy pilots and personalities. . . ."

Among these was Carol Burnett, perhaps the single happiest answer of her sex to the drought of laugh makers. Coming to the front via the Gary Moore TV Show, Miss Burnett gained the laughs and affections of millions by a welcome combination of irreverence for pomp and versatility of talent.

Miss Burnett originally came to New York from the West Coast, her eyes on the stage. But, given a chance by Moore, she soon became a TV fixture. Evidently doing what came naturally, she combined athletics, clowning, songs, dances. Her humor, above all else, was a determined foe of fraud.

As Neal Gilkyson Stuart pointed out in *The Ladies' Home Journal:* "If she wears a pretty dress, she confides, 'And I *smell* divine!' thus ruining the perfumed guile. If she wears a wig, it is invariably snatched off, revealing her own flattened hair beneath. Every crafty thought, base motive, ache of hangover and trembling hope is so pitiably naked that it commands excruciating sympathy.

" 'You are never going to forget tonight!' exclaims the handsome man as he lets her into his apartment.

" 'I'm not?' she gasps hopefully, and in two words exposes the poor palpitating heart of the healthy, lonely female. . . ."

When Jack Benny invited her to take part in a Tarzan-Jane TV routine on his television program, her first words were: "Gee, can I play Jane?"

Another bright comic following time tested laugh-making practices was the pliable Dick Van Dyke. That comedy pro from Sid Caesar's *Show of Shows,* Carl Reiner, conceived *The Dick Van Dyke Show,* wrote many of its scripts, was consultant when not writing them, and even slipped into some of them as a bit actor.

The show's supporting cast was well chosen, including veteran comedian Morey Amsterdam, present when television comedy was born; his partner, the former baby star of radio, Rose Marie; together with Mary Tyler Moore, who proved again that good looks need not be a barrier to good laugh-making.

One explanation of the Van Dyke success was his link with sound comic tradition. "I am a visual, physical comedian," Van Dyke said, "I still hate to get up alone. People think I'm a stand-up comic. I'm not."

Inspection of the Van Dyke show established the line of descent, not precise but unmistakable, from vigorous traditional American comedy. There was a live audience to, as Mary Tyler Moore put it, "tell us where the jokes are."

Van Dyke could take a prat fall with the best of the old timers, and there was a spontaneous quality reminiscent of Mack Sennett days. "Some of our funniest shows have come from our worst scripts," Van Dyke said.

Other laugh makers of the early 1960s carrying forward time-tested comic traditions included Jack E. Leonard, the veteran king of the "insult" comedians. Leonard was in the tradition of old burlesque-vaudeville laugh makers, often depending more on native wit and ability to ad lib humorous lines than on gag writers.

Leonard's forceful manner of delivering his jokes, coming from a man so big and uttered with such rapidity, took on a certain power, like a bowling ball that attains its greatest speed just before it knocks down the pins. Burt Boyar in *Esquire* magazine described Leonard as "undoubtedly the most imitated comedian in show business . . . Comedians will duel with him in private and among friends, but they prefer not to take their careers in their hands by crossing *words* with him on a stage or on TV."

Another popular comedian was Jerry Lewis, one of the few laugh makers of the era able to attract large audiences to motion picture theaters. "Although there has never been much question about Lewis' commercial standing as a film comedian," one critic stated, "there have always been reservations in sophisticated circles over his comic artistry and creativity." Although he leaned heavily on the obvious for his laughs, Lewis was essentially a physical comedian. Another was Buddy Hackett, heavy-set, rubbery-faced funnyman, whose questionable grammar hid a quick wit. A fellow comedian said of Hackett: "I think what's wrong with a lot of comedians today, including myself, is we don't have the ability to do the physical things, the physical comedy that Buddy can do. Buddy knows how to use his body and his face more than most comedians today."

A notable comic innovator was Ernie Kovacs whose death early in 1962 shocked the entertainment-loving nation. An advocate of zany sketches and wild gags, in his TV shows Kovacs constantly reached for ever wilder comic situations. Impatient with trying to fit old motion picture or radio techniques into the relatively new medium of television, Kovacs believed in experimentation. "There isn't anything that you can't make fun of if you want to," he said.

His humor was largely visual. He even began to produce complete TV shows entirely in pantomime, the only sound being classical music carefully selected to fit the mood of what he was trying to say. Under Kovacs' spell, painted portraits spoke; the water in a painted waterfall gurgled; a duck in a shooting gallery produced a gun from under its wing and shot back; a tense operating room closeup became, as the camera rolled back, a family carving a turkey.

In a commercial for a cigar company, Kovacs participated in a typical cowboy gun fight. After the shooting, he lit one of his huge cigars. Smoke poured out of him as though from a sieve.

"He found humor in everything in life, from gadgets . . . to stuffy social mores," commented Joe Hyams in the *New York Herald-Tribune*. "In whatever Kovacs did," wrote Jack Gould in *The New York Times,* "there was projected a wacky lilt and

Vaughn Meader, Bob Newhart, Nichols and May, Mort Sahl and Shelley Berman, all "stand-up" or "sit-down on a stove" comedians, brought a rebirth of satire.

For a time, night clubs were places where comedians could experiment with satire before live audiences. Scene is from off-Broadway night spot, The Premise Players, where spontaneity and the ad lib were a specialty of the house.

madness that somehow carried its own message of reassurance in today's stern and formalized world. Sometimes the Kovacs point of view was wildly hilarious, sometimes thoroughly puzzling, but there never was doubt about whose view it was."

Kovacs was one of the first comedians of the period who could be called a pioneer. He was not to be the last. As the 1960s developed, comedy increasingly reflected the need for topical comment and reaction to events of the day.

Among influences that helped encourage younger comedians were TV "host" programs. Ed Sullivan, who almost singlehandedly kept old-fashioned vaudeville abreast of the machine age, gave innumerable comedians their big chance. The Jack Paar TV show gave a helping hand to scores of laugh makers including Dick Gregory, Jack Carter, Hermione Gingold, Phyllis Diller, Nipsey Russell, Dody Goodman, Joey Bishop, Milt Kamen, Buddy Hackett, Dave Astor, Jonathan Winters, Cliff Arquette (Charlie Weaver), etc.

Paar himself tended to be more a master of ceremonies than professional funnyman. "Absolute honesty is important," Paar was quoted by *Television Magazine*. "Someone who is unreal, phony, shows through. You might fool the viewers once or twice, but you can't fool them for long." In an era of prepared scripts and frozen fun, Paar provided a rather welcome feeling of spontaneity and forthrightness. The human quality showed through more frequently on Paar's programs—even the commer-

There were many who laughed harder at Victor Borge's rare television "concerts" than at any other comedy act. Carol Burnett was one of the few comediennes who was consistently able to challenge male funnymen on the popularity scale.

cials—than on most others. And people seemed hungry for it. This may have accounted for the amazing fact that Paar accumulated on his late TV show some 164 participating television stations and a viewing audience approaching 3,000,000 steady followers with some 8,633,000 at peak.

Another skilled and sophisticated entertainer who pioneered as combined comedian and host was Steve Allen, who helped introduce scores of funnymen including Louis Nye, Bill Dana, the Smothers brothers, Joey Forman, Buck Henry, Tom Poston, Mort Sahl, Pepper and Davis, Don Knotts.

Still another pioneer was low pressure Dave Garroway, who for years woke people up on the *Today* show. "Don't tell lies to the people," was the way Garroway once explained his success. "If somebody doesn't show up, say he isn't here. If something goes wrong, admit it."

Successors to hosts such as Garroway and Paar were numerous in the years that followed: Merv Griffin, Joey Bishop, Johnny Carson, Dick Cavett, David Frost, Mike Douglas and more. Some gave part-time allegiance to serving as comedians. Others contributed to comedy mostly by giving young aspiring laugh makers their chance. Almost every comedian to come forward in this era was either born or developed on one or all of these "talk" shows.

During this period, TV variety shows were not the only vehicle giving comedians

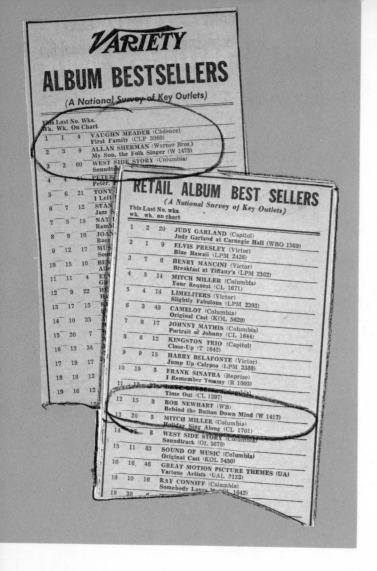

As the sale of record albums in the 1960's boomed, Vaughn Meader's comic imitation of President Kennedy broke all sales records. Bob Newhart's recordings achieved success almost overnight.

opportunity to be funny in public. There was also a rebirth of popularity of the old-fashioned phonograph record, new, unbreakable, long playing and of high fidelity.

According to Paul Kresh, a member of the National Academy of Recording Arts and Sciences, in the *American Record Guide:* "The growing list of comics on discs makes one wonder at times if they've all abandoned the borscht circuit, night clubs and TV channels for recording studios in order to preserve their art for posterity.

"They haven't, of course, and moreover they tend to bring these backgrounds right along with them. Some are subtle, some crass and vulgar, some cruel, some whimsical, some 'sick'; some understate, most overstate, and a few are just down-right, indefinably funny."

W. Schwann, Inc., publisher of the widely used long playing record catalog, points out that prior to 1960 it did not even include a special category of comedy records. The first listing included ninety-six records. The following year, in 1961, the number had jumped to 284 while in 1963 there were no less than 450 titles and the number rose steadily throughout the decade.*

* By the end of the 1960s the most productive comedy disc makers included: Moms Mabley, 19; Homer & Jethro, 15; Dewey Pigmeat Markham, 13; Jonathan Winters, 11; Brother Dave Gardner, 10; Allan Sherman, 8; Smothers Brothers, 7; Bill Cosby, 8; Lenny Bruce, 8; Shelley Berman, 7; Phyllis Diller, 7.

Steve Allen helped introduce many young comics to television audiences. Included was an off-beat team known as the Smothers Brothers.

Credit for the first hit comedy record of this decade generally is given to Andy Griffith, direct descendant of the Jonathan, country bumpkin type of comedian, whose *What It Was, Was Football* deserves rating both as a laugh classic and a pioneer. Other early discs include Stan Freburg's *St. George and the Dragonet* and Eddie Laurence's recording.

Comedy records were not exactly new. Edison's *Uncle Josh* series were popular decades ago as was Victor's famous *Cohen on the Telephone*. The comedians Moran and Mack, the *Two Black Crows,* made records that were big sellers. However, nothing has occurred in history that can equal the tremendous surge in popularity of the comedy records which started in the '60s. Records of Bob Newhart or Bill Dana (Jose Jiminez) were listed right up there with the records of Frank Sinatra, Harry Belafonte and Mitch Miller.

In discussing the matter on an *Open End* TV program, David Susskind asked, "How do you describe this kind of comedy?"

BOB NEWHART: I was surprised that my album did as well as it did. I thought it might be a fad with Shelley Berman, who really sold an awful lot of them. And now, I think it's a market, a definitely young adult market.

TOM POSTON: Mike Nichols and Elaine May album sold like a best seller album of music.

SUSSKIND: Why are people buying comedy albums?

ALAN KING: . . . You know the kids today are extremely bright, and they have a great sense of humor . . . but they can't afford to come to the Copacabana or the Latin Quarter or the Chez Paris in Chicago. So what do they do? They buy these albums. And they all get together in their apartment or their dormitory, and they open up a bottle of milk. And, they have an evening's entertainment . . .

Most people didn't know Bob Newhart existed until a phonograph record bearing his thin, nasal voice and his brand of subtle satire began to sell by the thousands in communities all over America.

Success came suddenly. The reward was national prominence. Newhart looked more as if he should be working in a bank or an insurance office than making people laugh for a living. Actually, he was an accountant.

Included among his best-known routines was an Abraham Lincoln sequence, having to do with an imaginary telephone conversation between Lincoln and his press agent. Basically it's the idea, Newhart explained, that if we had "today's science of advertising during the Civil War, and there was no Lincoln around, an ad man would have created a Lincoln out of whoever was in office. And he'd say things (in a one-way telephone conversation) like this:

Dick Gregory combined laugh making with a social conscience. "I began taking more and more time off from being a funnyman," he said, "to help my people."

Hi, ya, sweetheart, how's everything going? How was Gettysburg? Abe, listen, I got your note, what seems to be the problem? You're thinking of shaving it off? Abe, you're kidding, aren't you? Don't you see that that's part of the image? It's right, with a shawl, and a stovepipe hat. You don't have a shawl? Where did you leave the shawl this time, Abe? You left it in Washington? What are you wearing, Abe? A cardigan. Abe, don't you see that that doesn't fit with a stovepipe hat . . . Abe, trust in us on this—that's what you're paying us for. Abe, you got the speech? You haven't changed the speech, have you, Abe? Abe, why do you change the speeches? You typed it? Abe, how many times have we told you on the backs of envelopes, it will look ad lib, as if you wrote it on the way over. Abe, do the speech the way Charlie wrote it. The inaugural address won. Will you do it the way he wrote it? You talked to some newspaper men? I wish you wouldn't talk to newspaper men. You're always putting your foot—No, no, no, that is just what I am driving at, Abe, you're a railsplitter before you were an attorney. Abe, read the biography again.

Like many of the new comedians of the 1960's, Newhart had serious thoughts behind his comedy lines. In an interview by Pete Martin in *The Saturday Evening Post,* Newhart confessed some concern with his TV future.

"Those who control the medium are obsessed with the notion that if they offend even one viewer, they have one less customer. What the TV biggies don't know is that people like entertainment with bite. They want satire. The growth of talking-record sales proves that. When the public couldn't get satire on TV, it turned to records. Instead of half-hour shows and animated cartoons replacing Westerns, satire could be the next TV trend. . . ."

Another phenomenally successful laugh maker on records, this time a team, was Mike Nichols and Elaine May, who began as cabaret comedians. Highly gifted, they observed life about them and composed devastating satirical routines to expose folly and hypocrisy. "The role of the writer or artist is to be the competent observer," they said.

It was at the University of Chicago that the pair met, and according to them, "loathed each other on sight." Both were active in theatrical groups in Chicago and moved into night clubbing together, in New York and elsewhere.

After successful appearances, Steve Allen gave them a chance on his TV program, and later their appearances on *Omnibus* sealed their future. They were hits. In a sense, Nichols and May were the scientists of modern humorists. They probed deep into motivations, exposing to laughs the frailties and frauds they found, whether it was the overzealous mother who would not eat for days for fear her mouth would be full when her son called; the dentist who confessed his love for his patient; the name-dropping disc jockey who knew Bertrand Russell well; or the male patient who visited a lady doctor for the first time.

"Some people," said *The New Yorker,* "even find Nichols and May too precise to be funny at all, among them a number of ardent admirers who look upon the team less as entertainers than as important social critics, or even leaders of a crusade for a more decent world."

Allan Sherman and Vaughn Meader were two more sensationally successful come-

Jack Benny pictured before the junior high school that bears his name, built in Waukegan, Illinois, his birthplace. Bob Hope, the wealthiest comedian in history, received an honorary degree at Georgetown University in 1962. His advice to young people about to go out into the world was: "Don't go."

dians on records of the era. Sherman at first was a creator of laugh-making material for others, such as Joe E. Lewis and Jackie Gleason.

Respected as an ingenious "comedy brain," Sherman helped dream up an idea for a TV panel show in 1951. *I've Got a Secret* has been running ever since.

He tried on his own stuff just for size, and usually before small groups of friends. Known as a satirical funnyman in Hollywood circles, Sherman was not widely recognized until a Warner Brothers representative heard him put on his guitar song routine at a private party.

My Son, the Folk Singer resulted. Sherman used both his typewriter and his guitar, putting irreverent new lyrics to beloved old melodies. His first *My Son* record quickly

Red Skelton received an honorary degree from Emerson College, Boston, in 1961 which declared, "You have a sensitivity and concern for the burdens and suffering of your fellow man."

sold a million and zoomed to the top of the record hit parade. A sequel, *My Son, the Celebrity,* was also gobbled up by a public hungry for his kind of sophisticated humor.

If Sherman's records sold amazingly well, Vaughn Meader's laugh-making about the Kennedy family sold even better. People rushed to their nearest record store, demanding Meader's discs in such numbers that they had to be rationed. *The First Family* sold an all time high of over 4,500,000 platters, out-distancing not only Sherman, but also the one-time champion, *My Fair Lady.*

Meader, an unknown, youthful entertainer, had several strategic advantages working for him. First of all, he came from the Boston area and his tongue and ear needed little introduction to the speech habits of the natives there.

He also had the gift of perfect pitch which helped him listen to verbal mannerisms and mimic them with incredible skill. In addition, he had the help of Naomi Brossart, who mimicked the First Lady while Meader did the take-off on President Kennedy. Add to this combination the helping hand of capable gag writers, the *First Family* album sold 2,500,000 in the first four weeks and people were begging for more, which were rushed to the market from some ten record-making factories working overtime in various parts of the country.

People pleaded for the right to spend their money for an extra record for a friend; airplanes were used to rush batches of records to distributors; Republicans tried to

197

estimate whether Vaughn Meader's success was an asset or a liability; and so did the Democrats, who made the most of the traditional American ability to joke about the object of their affections.

For ten years Shelly Berman tried unsuccessfully to get a foothold in the serious theater. Then he turned to comedy. A successful appearance on Jack Paar's show helped send him on his way. In rapid succession came engagements at the Blue Angel in New York and then twelve shows for Ed Sullivan. Shelley now became a household name. He toured the night club circuit, setting attendance records at the Blue Angel, Mister Kelly's, the hungry i, the Venetian Room of the Fairmont Hotel in San Francisco, and the Empire Room of the Waldorf Astoria Hotel in New York. At each of the last two spots, he broke records held jointly by Harry Belafonte and Lena Horne. His recording, *Inside Shelley Berman,* sold in the hundreds of thousands and was the first non-musical album to be awarded the Gold Record. His other albums have earned additional honors.

Berman, who had helped open the record field for comedians, also blazed a trail for them on the concert stage. Travelling by plane, train and car, he covered hundreds of thousands of miles on three concert tours which attracted huge crowds in every section of the country. On one tour playing in twenty-seven cities, he set a mark for all to shoot at in one run of four performances at the Purdue University Field House in Lafayette, Indiana, where 26,435 people paid to see him. He was the first non-musical performer ever to appear at Chicago's famed Orchestra Hall.

Berman found comedy in ordinary frustrations of life about him: a telephone conversation with a child who keeps hanging up the phone, television commercials, a dentist ominously taking x-rays, the smile of an airplane stewardess.

Referring to the art of Shelley Berman, Louis Untermeyer, famous American poet and critic, stated, "Rarely in our history has there been so great a need for comedy. . . . Berman projects everyday occurrences so persuasively that little by little, line by line, laugh after laugh, they become excruciating. . . . He shares our confusions . . . and our bewilderments."

"I don't think it is my job to make a social comment," Berman once said. "If a social comment comes out of what I do, that's gravy. But it is not what I am after. . . . I am after laughs."

If Shelley Berman was not primarily interested in social comment, another comedian, who gained fame in the early '60's, Mort Sahl, was. Sahl was characterized as "one of the earliest ripples in the wave of cerebral American comics." Asked how he makes people laugh, Sahl answered: "I tell the truth and the people break up."

Of course, it was not quite that simple. Called the "thinking man's comedian," Sahl combined irreverence with willingness to tread little-walked paths in the area of topical comment.

His usual finish punch line in his monologues was the question, "Are there any groups that I have not offended?"

His technique was, as he said, a sort of flowing free association of ideas, carelessly (it would seem) linked together but actually interconnected with considerable care and artistry.

Time magazine, devoting a cover picture and several pages to Sahl, described his antics as a "revolt against pomposity." Indeed there could have been hardly a less pompous appearing person than the skinny, tieless Sahl, clad in a loose sweater, and nervously clutching a folded newspaper.

His appeal was intellectual; his approach topical; his source material usually the daily news.

Sahl began in the West coast night club, the hungry i, and moved to TV and recordings. He had the knack of amusing people in both high and low positions. Adlai Stevenson's appreciation of his quips was said to have helped rocket Sahl to prominence. Political leaders of all parties laughed at Sahl, although more Democrats laughed than Republicans.

Buddy Hackett said of Sahl that he was "not sick, he's aggressive." And aggressive he was. *The New Yorker* magazine once stated that Sahl was "against practically everything." Actually, Sahl disputed this, saying: "If I criticize somebody, it's only because I have higher hopes for the world, something good to replace the bad.

"People keep accusing me of being an intellectual," complained Sahl. "It is interesting that in the seven years I was at the University of California, no one called me that."

Sahl was innately controversial; a one-man reaction to the period of the mid-1950's, when nonconformity was sometimes considered subversive. As a matter of fact, the joke that set Sahl off on his night club career had to do with a coat he described as a "McCarthy jacket."

"It is like an Eisenhower jacket," he quipped, "except it has an extra zipper to go across the mouth."

"The news of such audacity at such a time," wrote *The New Yorker*, "rapidly reached the campuses in the San Francisco area." In no time at all the West coast youth had a new hero.

In a guest appearance with Steve Allen on John McCaffery's TV show, *The Nation's Future,* Sahl said:

I took my life and put it on the block in clubs with an audience to find out whether they were listening. All the time the mass media were saying, 'You cannot joke about President Eisenhower,' I was joking about him. All the time they said, 'You cannot joke about Senator McCarthy,' I was joking about him. And I don't think I was on a prison talent show, either.

Another comedian of the new type and new era was Dick Gregory. A sit-down or stand-up, cigarette-smoking comedian out of Chicago, Gregory was sometimes referred to as "the black Mort Sahl."

"In the Congo," replied Gregory, "Mort Sahl would be referred to as the white Dick Gregory!"

A few years before Gregory was washing cars during the day to augment his show business income. His rise to fame was one of the sensational successes of the entertainment industry. Gregory also depended on the day's news for ammunition, carefully studying the newspapers and magazines before each performance.

The story is that Gregory made his first major appearance in the Playboy Club in

Peter Sellers

Phil Silvers

Buddy Hackett

Ernie Kovacs

Carl Reiner

George Gobel

Mickey Rooney

Imogene Coca

Shirley Booth

Jackie Leonard

Martha Raye

Henry Morgan

Hermione Gingold

Sam Levenson

Tony Randall

Jerry Lewis

Wally Cox

Peter Ustinov

Chicago when the main comedian failed to show up. That evening a convention of business executives from the South was present. There was some hesitation before Gregory was permitted to go on.

He began something like this:

Ladies and gentlemen, I understand there are a good many Southerners in the room tonight. I know the South very well. I spent twenty years there one night. . . . It is dangerous for me to go back. You see . . when I drink I think I am Polish. . . . One night, I got so drunk I moved out of my own neighborhood. . . . The last time I was down South, I walked into this restaurant and this waitress came up to me and said, 'We don't serve colored people in here.' 'That's all right,' I said, 'I don't eat them, bring me a whole fried chicken instead.'

And so Gregory carried on his deceptively mild mannered way. When he was finished, so the story goes, the audience rose in applause and several members invited him South to entertain their friends.

Gregory had a sly humor which sneaked up on the listener when least expected: "The way things are . . . ten years from now, you'll have to be my color to get a job. . . . I am really for Abraham Lincoln. If it hadn't been for Abe, I would still be on the open market . . . I sat at a lunch counter for nine months. They finally integrated and didn't have what I wanted . . ."

"They are making a picture called Stagecoach South . . . They offered me the leading part and I turned it down, because I know the first time they make a Negro Western, the Indians gonna win . . . When I do land on the moon, a six-legged, green-skinned man is sure to come up and tell me he don't want me marrying his sister."

Gregory invaded the Southland in 1963 to lend the influence of his name on the side of people demonstrating for equality. In Greenwood, Mississippi, the United Press International reported, "Police manhandled comedian Dick Gregory when he and other Negroes refused orders to disperse a voter registration march to the voting booths."

In Birmingham, Alabama, a few weeks later, Gregory again joined demonstrators for equal rights and was jailed together with a large number of others including hundreds of children.

"We're glad this city doesn't have enough jails or enough police brutality to go around," Gregory commented from jail. "There are all kinds of hunting licenses and seasons for wild game," he said, "but it's open season on us—Negroes—24 hours a day."

Dick Nolan in the *San Francisco Examiner* claimed at the time that Gregory was a double-edged disappointment. "He is a disappointment to the hot-eyed radicals of the left. He is a disappointment to the cold-hearted radicals of the right. But to an American thirsting for laughs, Gregory 'represents a new voice' in the ranks of comedians—the first major Negro laugh maker since Bert Williams."

In a few brief years, a changing Dick Gregory was to herald a dramatic change in much of American comedy.

15

The Comedian: Barometer
of National Health

In the 1970's, comedy became—in addition to entertainment—increasingly an instrument of political and social commentary.

Not that all funny men turned to current events for ammunition. Many—among them Red Skelton, Lucille Ball, Jerry Lewis, Jack Benny and Jimmy Durante—continued comedy as usual. "Songs is my forty," said Jimmy. "Wid a couple a jokes, a couple a gals in da act—what else am I gonna do? Best t'ing for me is ta jest be me."

But numerous laugh makers were finding popularity, particularly among youth, in a "comedy of dissent." According to Steve Allen, "There is a generation of angry young men. Youth is revolting all over the world, and all the world is in ferment, and I think this is simply reflected in humor. It is reflected in art, poetry, tailoring and all sorts of things."

The silent generation of the 1950's was indeed giving way to the irreverent generation of the 1960's and 1970's. Arthur Gelb of *The New York Times* called the new crop of comedians "modern evangelists. . . . The keynote of their satire is iconoclasm; they are out to shock people into an awareness of what is going on around them."

Contributing to the rapid spread of the new comedy was, of course, the all-persuasive influence of television. By 1969, most American homes used television more than five hours a day, and the figure was going up! "The average child, before he enters first grade," said an F.C.C. commissioner, "spends more time in front of the TV set than he will getting his B.A. degree."

When cowboys took over television entertainment in the 1950s and early 1960s, comedians took flight. And when the rage for boots and spurs began to abate, the spy season opened. An epidemic of intrigue, violence and sex became standard television fare.

However, as the years passed, a return to comedy, both sophisticated and unsophisticated, took place. But more often than not, it was a different kind of laugh making: topical, angry, often shocking. Whether the medium was television, stage, screen or records, comedians increasingly were reflecting a world around them knee deep in crises.

Pat Paulsen, who possessed "The deadest pan since Buster Keaton," ran for the Presidency in 1968 on a peace platform. "Let them sell guns, but no bullets," was his answer to the gun control issue.

The Smothers Brothers developed into one of television's most politically outspoken comedy acts. "We stand out," said Tom Smothers, "because nothing is being said. We would be moderates anywhere else."

David Susskind, who had been one of the few important figures in the entertainment world to stand up against the influence of McCarthyism, commented: "Slowly and often imperceptibly, our mass entertainment media are beginning to take on some of the urgent responsibilities of our times."

"Comedy is not an isolated thing," said Milt Kamen, standup comedian. "It is something that has to do with our daily lives, the whole country's life, the world's life."

So there began to appear, from sunrise programs to night clubs, a rebirth of topical humor—but often with a shocking irreverence hitherto unknown.

Mimics of famous political personalities found appreciative audiences. David Frye was one who demonstrated amazing ability to imitate and exaggerate voices and facial expressions of those he would hold up to ridicule. "People long to laugh at their leaders," he was quoted as saying. "Audiences need a way to vent their feelings and fears about these big, political figures, and they can do it with me. . . ."

Politics and comedy mixed when David Frye did his imitations of Richard Nixon and Lyndon B. Johnson. When a Presidential candidate in 1968, Dick Gregory pledged that his "foreign aid program will mainly consist of sending money and food to needy people in foreign lands—like Mississippi and Alabama."

One of television's more off-beat popular comedy shows: Dan Rowan's and Dick Martin's *Laugh-In* featuring Goldie Hawn, successor to Gracie Allen's comic laurel; Arte Johnson, sinister German soldier and dirty old man; Theresa Graves; Henry Gibson; Alan Sues, Joanne Worley, Ruth Buzzi, etc.

One of his typical parodies was an imitation of George Wallace, former governor of Alabama: "I have a majority of the uncommitted voters. I also have a lot of the voters who have already been committed. These ah ma people! I am heah to say that I am sick and tard of looters and rioters. Last week they burned down ma library in Alabama—both books, one I ain't even colored yet."

Another comedian to win popularity by caricature was Don Adams in the television serial *Get Smart*. As the bumbling secret agent, Adams evidently supplied viewers with welcome relief from the hordes of implausible spies that had descended upon them. Another foe of pomposity and fraud was Pat Paulsen, sad-eyed comedian, whose vague resemblance to a basset hound masked skillful comedy techniques.

Paulsen achieved national recognition on the *Smothers Brothers Comedy Hour,* where his ironic "editorials" helped him steal part of the show from better-known comedians. Paulsen's sensitive timing permitted even doubtful jokes to seem hilarious. Claiming to have been a school-boy athlete, Paulsen would solemnly inform his TV audience that "in high school, I was a four letter word."

His ridiculous but seemingly sage editorial advice was listened to eagerly by millions of television viewers. "I am opposed to sex education in the schools," he once said. "Let kids today learn it where we did—in the gutter."

Discussing the rumor of his possible candidacy for the Presidency, Paulsen declared: "I have not only denied it to national audiences on television, but spent considerable time and expense travelling around the country, visiting and subsidizing groups of loyal supporters who deny it too."

In what was described as "the most unusual Presidential campaign the United States has ever known," Paulsen promised his followers that, no matter what the

Too rarely have films achieved high levels of comedy in the 1960's and early 1970's. Among recent all-time box-office hits were: *It's a Mad, Mad, Mad, Mad World; The Graduate;* and *The Russians are Coming, The Russians are Coming.*

outcome of the election, he would remain "a common, ordinary, simple savior of America's destiny."

The weekly show that gave Paulsen his big chance, the *Smothers Brothers Comedy Hour,* itself marked something of a milestone in modern American comedy. While Tom and Dick Smothers had achieved a reputation for their particular brand of fun making, it was only in the period of the late 1960's that the brothers began veering sharply toward the area of political commentary. Perhaps it was because they were young and the youth of America lacked spokesmen on television networks. Perhaps it simply was the fact that the brothers felt strongly about current issues. At any event, the Smothers brothers humor increasingly involved "controversial" issues and entertainers of the day.

"The young generation is talking," said Tom Smothers. "The question is, is anybody listening?"

In the spring of 1969, a CBS announcement was made that the *Smothers Brothers Comedy Hour* had been cancelled. A network spokesman stated: "The central issue involved here is whether a broadcast organization has some responsibility to the public with respect to questions of taste. . . ."

Stated Tom Smothers: "While our cities burn, young people watch documentaries on the efficacy of our government. . . ."

Another comedian candidate for the Presidency of the United States in 1968 was Dick Gregory who claimed that if elected, "my foreign aid program would mainly

Jonathan Winters was one of the most gifted of modern satirists. His versatility caused him to be called the "one man repertory company."

Zero Mostel, one of the more creative of modern comedians, believes that, "The free-dom of any society varies with the size of its laughter." Bill Cosby became the first black entertainer with a regular starring role in a television series.

consist of sending money and food to needy people in foreign lands—like Mississippi and Alabama."

The Dick Gregory of the late 1960's and early 1970's was somewhat different from the earlier night club entertainer, in addition to longer hair and a beard. More mili-tant, more insistent upon bringing forward issues which he felt vital, Gregory largely gave up the night club for engagements on college and university campuses.

Asked by Larry Wilde, author of a study of comedians, whether the Negro has a different sense of humor from the white man, Gregory answered: "Oh, yes, because the Negro has a different set of values than the white man. The white man lacks humor. . . . We laugh at him. . . . We have been laughing at him for years. Every-thing he seems to do we think is silly. We go to the Negro movie house, you think the Negro is loud, boisterous, ignorant and uncouth, but he is not. . . . He is laugh-ing at white folks. His biggest form of entertainment has been the American white man. . . ."

If Dick Gregory became the most widely known black comedian since Bert Wil-liams, he was merely the first of a growing number of nationally known black laugh makers, who gained prominence in this era. In reality, many Negro comedians were

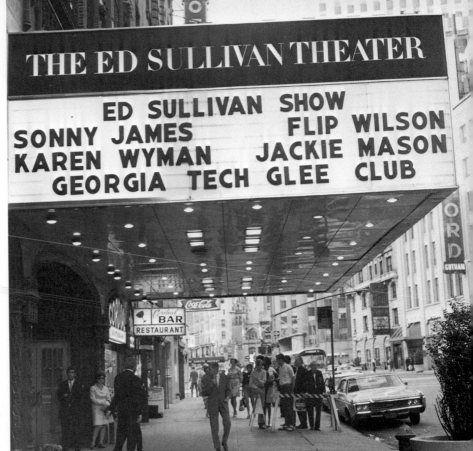

The *Ed Sullivan Show*, television's perpetual gift to vaudeville, for years supplied one of the few consistent outlets for new comedy talent.

new only to whites. "The line that leads to Moms Mabley, Nipsey Russell, Dick Gregory, Bill Cosby and myself," stated Godfrey Cambridge, talented black laugh maker, "can be traced back to the satire of slave humor, back even through minstrelsy. . . ."

Cambridge pointed out how around the 1940 era, large numbers of black families came from the South to northern urban centers. Black entertainers became more frequent and black comedians "were speaking more and more the common, inside humor of the streets. . . . For the first time, a Negro comedian became a hero. . . . All of a sudden, there was no more shuffle. . . ."

An increasing number of white people began to understand that, "The ability to laugh heartily," in the words of James Weldon Johnson, famed black poet, "is in part the salvation of the American Negro. The Negro's knack of making his white owner laugh is the basis for black survival during the days of slavery." It was also the basis for a vital brand of laugh making which the black entertainer was to contribute in the modern era. Another of the more popular black comedians was Flip Wilson, whose casual laugh making hid a carefully structured technique. "Do you want to build a $50,000 home and some Indian build a wigwam next to it?" he would

Mary Tyler Moore

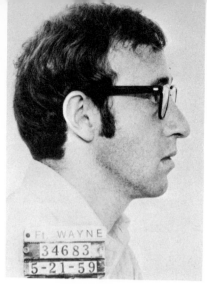

Woody Allen

Flip Wilson

ask his audience. "I never heard of anybody playing cowboys and colored people."

For decades, some of the nation's most able comedians seldom were known beyond Harlem and other ghetto areas. Among these was Moms Mabley, black comedienne, who late in life became a popular national entertainer on television and on records.

Once asked how she goes about her laugh making, Moms replied: "I just tell folks the truth. If they don't want the truth, then don't come to Moms. Anybody that comes to me, I'll help 'em. I don't say anything I don't mean."

Still another prominent comedian of the 1970's was Bill Cosby, the first black entertainer to have a featured role in a regular television program. "My whole career took a big turn from the time Dick Gregory made it five or six years ago," Cosby stated. An athlete in school, Cosby found he had a natural inclination toward comedy, but more important than that, an intimate knowledge of ordinary people, particularly the underprivileged. Cosby was able to provide a special, gentle type of humor, both satirical and understanding at the same time.

The new comedy—black and white—gave birth to one of television's most successful shows in *Laugh-In,* a weekly collection of rapid fire satire and lunacy.

Laugh-In was a frenetic successor to *This Was The Week That Was,* which engaged in effective political satire before its sudden curtailment a few years previous. *Laugh-In* provided television comedy with one of its more creative technological approaches since the days of Ernie Kovacs. A mixture of physical comedy and social comment, the review rushed through its weekly hour so breathlessly that it was difficult to recall what happened when it was all over.

Joke followed upon joke at such a pace that, if the viewer missed one, he need not worry; another would be along any second. That is not to say that all or even most of the jokes had merit; it simply did not seem to matter.

Laugh-In made use, to an unprecedented extent, of cutting-room techniques to avoid boredom and to leave the viewer hungry for more. The show bore a resemblance to a sophisticated, many ringed circus. Winner of six Emmy awards, Dan Rowan

Jack Lemmon

Richard Pryor

Alan King

Don Adams

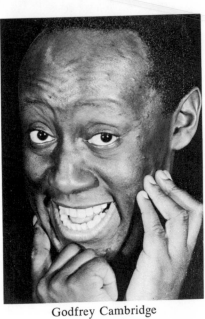

Godfrey Cambridge

Moms Mabley

Phyllis Diller

Anne Meara and Jerry Stiller

Don Rickles

Perhaps a reason why Charlie Chaplin remained popular with younger generations was that his comedy gave expression to what was on many a youthful mind: "More than machinery, we need humanity," he said. "More than cleverness, we need kindness and gentleness. . . . We want to live by each other's happiness—not by each other's misery. We don't want to hate and despise one another. In this world, there is room for everyone. And the good earth is rich and can provide for everyone."

and Dick Martin, part owners of *Laugh-In,* evidently believed there was safety in speed. For once, the commercials supplied a welcome moment of relative sanity.

The success of such television fare explained the growing plight of those night clubs that flourished during the era when meaningful laugh making was a TV rarity. Art D'Lugoff, proprietor of The Village Gate in New York, pointed to "the tremendous impact of television, both on the audience and on the performer. . . . If the performer is even mildly successful in a live situation, he is immediately swept up by the tube. . . ."

Another well-known night club, the hungry i, in San Francisco, also had its troubles. "Unable to beg, borrow or steal top talent (or audiences) away from television," stated *The New York Times* report, "this hallowed, north beat cellar has been forced to close its doors."

"This whole country is coming apart at the seams," stated Enrico Banducci, owner of the hungry i. "Nobody laughs any more. If they do, it is in front of the television set."

The rewards of television have not only tempted comedians from night clubs. "Comedy is now non-existent in practically all standard burlesque theaters," stated *Variety,* "for the very good reason that the shows no longer have any comedians, good or bad, only strippers, good or bad."

Television was also the culprit behind the holocaust that hit Hollywood years ago. People simply found it more convenient and cheaper to sit at home and laugh at television comedians than paying at a motion picture box office. Struggling for its existence, the movies responded by seeking a specialized field, difficult for the home television to match. They found it, more or less, in violence and sex.

While there have been successful film comedies in the 1960 and 1970 era, the list of *Variety's* "All Time Box Office Champs," contains significantly few modern films that owed their success primarily to laugh makers. Television, inevitably, had similar influence on the legitimate theater, largely represented by Broadway and off-Broadway productions. Interestingly, Mike Nichols and Elaine May, one time hilarious record-making comedy team, acting independently, had a finger in a number of productions in the theater and motion pictures. Another one of the rare success-ful producers of comedy, Neil Simon, indicated the trend toward content on Broadway:

"Humor isn't anything if it can't make you think and feel," he stated in *News-week.* "Anyone can make a baby laugh by shaking a rattle in its face. I don't want to write for infants and shake rattles."

Thus, if the living theater had its share of comedy, it was largely based upon the talent of its writers rather than the personality of its comedians.

Television not only captured most of the talented comedians of the period, but also subtley influenced not only the content of their humor, but also their very technique of laugh making. For example, the coming of the "stand-up" comedian was largely the result of the limits of television. At first, more or less the prisoner of the microphone, the stand-up comic employed minimum help from costume, setting or physical antics—but depended mostly on verbal jokes and his ability to tell them.

Another phenomenon of television, applying particularly but by no means exclusively to the stand-up comedian, was the strategic role behind the scenes of the comedy writer.

Of course, the comic writer has always been of considerable, if unappreciated, importance to the comedian. While certain laugh makers, such as Fred Allen, wrote much of their own material, an increasing number have depended upon gag writers. For years, Bob Hope was one of the nation's most celebrated comedians by virtue of his rapid-fire delivery, an accomplishment not only based upon his own special brazen talent as a stand-up comedian, but also the result of those who prepared his often side-splitting commentary. When asked once who was the most influential person in her life, Lucille Ball thought briefly and replied: "My writers."

Once when confronted in public by the sharp wit of Fred Allen, Jack Benny replied: "You wouldn't say that if my writers were here."

The physical comedian, the circus clown, the laugh maker who depends largely upon the accompaniment of music or his ability at acrobatics, had less need for gag writing assistance. However, with the increasing disappearance of this type of comedy, the gag writer has evolved as perhaps the single most important factor in the success or failure of much of comedy today.

If television has extended its influence into almost every area of comedy, there is one region that it has not—and for good reasons—exerted as much influence. This is the area of what some call "sick" laugh making. Whether television standards will be changed in the future, it cannot be said. Nevertheless, up to the beginning of the 1970's, television had considered itself primarily family entertainment, as far as comedy was concerned anyway. Hence, the sick jokes which invaded the theater, the records and the night clubs were largely off the air waves. Nevertheless, they comprised a significant influence on American comedy. "Sex is no longer a taboo topic," stated *Time* magazine as early as 1966. "It is, in fact, one of the commonest. Humor has not only been firmly entrenched in the bedroom, but is increasingly being brought into the bathroom."

Speaking of the trend toward sick comedy, Alan King, the comedian, stated: "I wasn't so shocked at the comedian or what he was saying. I was shocked at the audience laughing at what he was saying. That's what frightened me. That there is a market for this. They talk about cave-ins and atomic fall-out. A man can say anything he wants, but there has to be a market in order for him to succeed. The fact that sick comics are succeeding today . . . that's what frightens me!"

One of the most successful and probably most talented of the so-called "sick" comedians was Lenny Bruce. According to Ralph J. Gleason, editor of *Jazz*, Bruce was actually a voice "dissenting from a world gone mad. . . . His colossal irreverence punctures the hypocrisy of religion, politics and other areas with an arrow tipped with poison."

When Bruce was hauled into court for using obscenity in public entertainment, the prosecution based its case on the argument that the purpose of comedy was to get laughs, and that Bruce's performance wasn't funny, and that Bruce simply had

218

indulged in the use of obscenity for obscenity's sake. The defense, which won acquittal, produced witnesses who testified that Bruce's work on the stage had "redeeming social significance," and that an obscene word had to be considered in this context and not in isolation.

The debate over the legitimacy of "sick" humor has involved numerous people in the entertainment industry. "I hear more sick humor," stated Mort Sahl, "from normal, responsible people than I hear from comedians. . . . People have to demand more from their comedians. . . ."

Commenting on trends in entertainment, Groucho Marx once stated: "I don't think you have to show love making on the screen any more than you have to show bowel movements. . . . When I heard about 'Hair,' I was kind of curious about the six naked primates on stage," Groucho stated in a *New York Times* interview, "so I called at the box office, and they said that tickets were $11 apiece. That's an awful price to pay. I went to my bathroom at home, took off my clothes and looked at the mirror for five minutes, and I said, 'This isn't worth $11.' "

"One thing that annoys me," stated Steve Allen, "is this exclusivity you are supposed to feel about comedy. People ask me if I think Lenny Bruce is funnier than W. C. Fields. Why choose? Why can't a person like them both? If I laugh at Red Skelton, I am not supposed to laugh at Mort Sahl. That doesn't make sense. . . ."

Regardless of taste in comedy—always a sensitive area—one fact is indisputable: there have been changes. According to Abel Green, veteran *Variety* editor, "No question that today's comedy is less physical and more cerebral. No question that the Will Rogers' brand of 'topics' from the headlines, presumably gauged at the lofty Ziegfeld Review trade, has long since been multiplied by dozens of equally effective comedians . . . for much wider appreciation. Many a latter day Negro comedian also is as flip and savvy as any of the other stand-up funsters. . . ."

But what are young people of today saying about comedy? What are they laughing at?

"Old humor is in great demand," wrote an editor of the *Daily Californian* in Berkeley. ". . . A mass, very large, of persons eagerly digest . . . Hollywood's poison each evening at the commercial run movie houses . . . And a much smaller, but surprisingly large body . . . dig the old masters of the screen. . . . We all like to laugh —a lot."

According to an editor of the *Yale Daily News,* the young people of today in large numbers "disdain comedy situations that pretend to be real, pretend to be the way everybody lives, they dislike canned laughter, and they enjoy comedy—like Chaplin and Fields—where the laugh making device is obvious." In other words, the Yale editor has the belief that comedy that attracts young people today in large numbers must not be fraudulent.

But regardless of the taste in humor, as the *Daily Californian* editor stated: "We all like to laugh—a lot. At least my friends and I work at it—often. I think we all do. . . . It draws us closer. . . ."

It has been said that the most important function of humor is to render a man more compassionate and understanding of his fellow man. Indeed, it is difficult to be hostile and humorous at the same time.

Mark Twain put the matter this way:

"The human race, in its poverty, has unquestionably one really effective weapon —laughter. . . . Against the assault of laughter, nothing can stand."

"Good night, folks, and good night, Mrs. Calabash, wherever you are."

Acknowledgments

Writing about comedy is a serious affair. The most liberal reader and broad-minded critic can become relentless when their standards of humor are violated. And violate them we have. Space alone made this necessary. Since there were judgments to be made, we made them. For such judgments, kindly blame us; not the following, whose counsel, assistance and encouragement we appreciate.

Among the people who helped were Mrs. Annie Stein, Abel Green, Harold Lloyd, Ed Wynn, Steve Allen, Mack Sennett, Sam Levenson, Harry Birdoff, Norman Franklin, Richard Maney, Sol Jacobson, Sally Powers, and many others.

Hundreds of books and countless periodicals and newspapers were, naturally, consulted in putting together this work. Among those books which, in retrospect, appear to have been most useful are included: *Show Biz* by Abel Green and Joe Laurie, Jr., Henry Holt & Company, New York, 1942; *The Merry Partners, the Age and Stage of Harrigan and Hart,* by E. J. Kahn, Jr., Random House, N. Y., 1955. *Weber and Fields,* by Felix Isman, Boni & Liveright, N. Y., 1924; *King of Comedy,* by Mack Sennett, Doubleday & Company, Garden City, 1954; *My Life is in Your Hands,* by Eddie Cantor, Harper & Bros., New York, 1928; *Schnozzola,* by Gene Fowler, The Viking Press, New York, 1951; *George M. Cohan,* by Ward Moorehouse, J. B. Lippencott Company, Philadelphia, 1943; *Charlie Chaplin,* by Theodore Huff, Abelard-Schuman, Ltd., New York, 1951; *Will Rogers,* by P. J. O'Brien, John C. Winston Company, Philadelphia, 1935; *W. C. Fields,* by Robert Lewis Taylor, Doubleday & Company, Garden City, 1949; *The Marx Brothers,* by Kyle Crichton, Doubleday & Company, Garden City, 1950; *Life With Groucho,* by Arthur Marx, Popular Library, New York, 1955; *Nigger,* by Dick Gregory, Pocket Books, New York, 1965; *The Great Comedians Talk about Comedy,* Larry Wilde, The Citadel Press, 1968; *Sixty Years of American Humor,* edited by Joseph Lewis French, Little Brown & Company, Boston, 1924; *The Treasurer's Report,* by Robert Benchley, Harper & Brothers, New York, 1930.

Bob Newhart's Lincoln sequence is reprinted by courtesy of Armanco Productions, Inc.

The extract on p. 107 is from *Charlie Chaplin* by Theodore Huff, Abelard-Schumann, Ltd. Copyright 1951 by Mr. Huff.

The extract on p. 142 is from *The Treasurer's Report* by Robert Benchley, Harper & Brothers. Copyright 1930 by Robert Benchley.

Picture acknowledgments are due many sources including among the most helpful:

Culver, 78, 136
Van Damm, 68, 128 (bottom right)
Museum of Modern Art, 72, 73, 84, 85, 90, 92, 93, 94, 97, 99, 100, 105, 107, 108, 113, 115
Brooklyn Dodger Baseball Club, 142
Ringling Brothers Barnum and Bailey, 139
William Morris Agency, 138 (top)
Walt Disney Prod., 122
Franklin D. Roosevelt Memorial Library, 102
National Van Lines, 91
Blair Publishing Co., 42
Little Church Around the Corner, 36
Library of Congress, 18, 26, 75
New York Public Library, 2, 8, 16, 23, 25 (top), 29, 34, 38, 43, 45, 46, 47, 50, 58, 64, 66, 68, 69, 76, 95, 96 (top), 98, 104, 106, 110, 118, 122, 126, 127, 128 (bottom left), 131, 137, 170
Museum of the City of New York, 14 (lower left), 19, 38, 44, 49, 56, 84
Wide World Photos, Inc., 74
Brooklyn Public Library, 22
Harvard Library, 25 (bottom)
Gjon Mili, 132
National Broadcasting Company, 59, 60, 67, 129, 138, 159, 160, 161, 162, 163, 164, 165, 167, 170, 173
Columbia Broadcasting System, 166
Metro-Goldwyn-Mayer, 117, 148, 149, 151, 154 (middle left)
Warner Brothers, 80, 146, 124
Columbia Pictures Corp., 154 (lower right), 158
Paramount Pictures Corp., 81, 116, 152, 156, 168 (top)
Twentieth-Century-Fox, 92 (lower), 120 (top), 150
Universal Picture Co., Inc., 78, 120 (left bottom), 154 (middle right), 157
Waukegan *News-Sun* (Jack Benny), 200
Max Waldman (Zero Mostel), 214
Playboy, 198
Richard Avedon (Nichols and May), 7
Sheldon Secunda, 194
UNICEF (Danny Kaye) Jacket and, 153
Rogers and Cowan, Inc. (Mort Sahl), 192

About the Author

WILLIAM CAHN, a graduate of Dartmouth College, is a public relations consultant and author of many successful books including the biography of Jimmy Durante, *Good Night, Mrs. Calabash, the secret of Jimmy Durante;* and the biography of Harold Lloyd, *Harold Lloyd's World of Comedy.*

His *The Laugh Makers, a pictorial history of American comedians,* is considered a definitive work on American comedy entertainers in America. It has been widely used in schools around the country.

Among Mr. Cahn's fifteen books have been a number of corporate histories as well as biographies of Van Cliburn and Albert Einstein. His greatest love, however, is in presenting the laugh makers of America, both past and present, because he is convinced that humor not only entertains, but also instructs and inspires.

Mr. Cahn is married and has three children and lives in New Haven, Connecticut.